BOSS It Up, Babe!

The Complete Guide to Crushing Your Personal Brand, Owning Your Online Space & Attracting Your Ideal Avatar

"For I know the plans I have for you, plans to prosper you and not to harm you, plans to give you hope and a future."

~ Jeremiah 29:11

Kimberly Olson, PhD

1

BOSS It Up, Babe!

The Complete Guide to Crushing Your Personal Brand, Owning
Your Online Space & Attracting Your Ideal Avatar

Copyright © 2021 by Kimberly Olson

Cover Designed by Olivia Windorf

All rights reserved.

www.TheGoalDiggerGirl.com

ISBN- 978-1-7327828-6-0

CONTENTS

FORWARD

In the first moment I connected with her, I asked, "So, do you go by Kim or Kimberly?" Immediately, confidently, and boldly she said with some fierce swag, "Oh, it's Kimberly." It was that moment that I intuitively knew... I had just met a BOSS.

Let's be super honest. So many people, especially people of the internet, throw around the word "Boss" like it's a name tag. What does it mean to truly be a boss? And not just a boss, a *woman boss* in the modern world leading the paths for so many other women to take charge and gain financial freedom in their lives? I'll tell you what it means. It means discipline. It means drive. It means dedication. It's perseverance, inward honesty, overcoming doubts, and difficult confrontations. It's setting the standard, leading by example with eyes on you always. It's creating a ripple effect, leaving a legacy, and shining your light so bright that others can find their way to their own potential. That's just what basic bosses do. You know you're in the presence of a legit boss when she does all of that, and at the same time, be humble, genuine, and *HILARIOUS AF* to own her authentic, badass-self, and show up to the world on social media dancing like no one (yet everyone) is watching. She does all this to show other women what real freedom and empowerment looks like. It's doing all that while taking the prestigious title of "Mom" to two little girls as well. Yeah, now that's a BOSS... and that my dear friends, and soon to be readers, is the magic of Kimberly Olson.

It still makes me laugh after I run out of breath as I introduce Kimberly as a guest speaker on my podcast or on a special training running through all her achievements and credentials. I mean WOW! PHDs, top 50 podcast host, best-selling author, TEDx speaker, has multiple streams of income and is debt free. What I find most important and impressive though is her drive to fulfill her passion. She has a burning desire to help women claim their power, pursue their dreams, and own the life that is calling to them. It is obvious why she is known as "The Goal Digger Girl". She embodies her brand. It's more than just her brand. It's who she is.

If this book is here in your hands now, there is no such thing as *coincidence*. It's not "woo-woo", it's physics. And Lord knows Kimberly and I love "woo-woo". You see, your vibration is in alignment with Kimberly's energy. Here's the thing, in BOSS It Up, Babe, you will learn techniques and strategies, but most importantly, you are plugging into the power of a woman who did it and continues to shine as #2 in the WORLD for recruiting in her network marketing company while owning a MULTI-7 figure coaching company (notice my emphasis with CAPS). You see, as a MULTI 7 figure sales producer myself, I know a Boss when I see one.

Kimberly is a BOSS.

She knows the ins-and-outs like the back of her hand and is ready to teach those who are willing to listen. What I love most about Kimberly, though, is that she knows who she is and simultaneously honors her journey of BECOMING.

No matter where you are on your journey, a whole new path can start NOW. You just need to be vulnerable and willing to take a step forward each and every day just how she does, how I do, and how every woman who wants to fulfill her purpose does. So, connect with the burning in your heart, know that you can because women like Kimberly are paving the path, and be grateful that she is here making that path clear. 'BOSS It Up, Babe' provides so much clarity for the woman who is ready to own her greatness. The strategies laid out in this book are here to help you to go faster, go bigger, and help you to create leaps and bounds as the BOSS in your own business.

PLEASE notice how Kimberly reiterates the importance of imperfect action throughout this book. I, as well, cannot speak to this enough. Every move forward results in growth. Even if it's not the "perfect" move forward. If you continue to move forward everyday, you will gain momentum. If you do not quit, you will not fail. Because truly, it's not WHAT you do everyday, it's WHO you are when you do it. You are not just the BOSS in your business, you are the BOSS of your life. And I cannot think of a better role model, mentor, coach, and BOSS Babe that leads by example other than Kimberly.

I am grateful to call Kimberly my friend, and my soul sister. Her honesty, her heart, her passion for life, her business, and her desire to help YOU are laid out with love on all these pages. Take it in. Read it over and over. To master your craft, it's not about reading several books, it's about reading one book several times. This is how you become an expert. And after reading this book numerous times myself, I can tell you, this is the ONE to read.

You CAN do this. You WILL do this. In fact, it's already done!

Just remember to…

Acknowledge It. Embrace It. See It Through.

And most importantly…BOSS It Up, Babe!

Cynthia Stant

CEO and Founder of the Spiritual Success Experience, Host of the Spiritual Success Podcast

GOAL DIGGER DEDICATION

At the core of any lofty goal is always a big reason to accomplish it. My biggest reason is, and always has been, my family. My husband, Scott, and my daughters, Addison and Elise, are my everything. They constantly cheer me on and they are the ones that keep me going. Thank you for loving me unconditionally!

Behind the scenes of our brand is a powerhouse of incredible women that have become like sisters to me. Anna Barefield is affectionately known as my #WorkWife and has been with me since day one. She oversees everything as President of The Goal Digger Girl. You ever wonder how we keep all the plates spinning? It's because of magical unicorn powers.

Our other right-hand ladies are Steph Dakin, Client Experience Director, and Allyson Mancini, Community Relations Manager. Steph interfaces with all our students in our programs and produces our content on multiple platforms. Allyson manages our Facebook™ Group community and oversees the wellness aspect too. These ladies create the high-vibe energy you can tangibly feel with all that we do as a company.

The Goal Digger Girl brand is only three years old, but we've experienced a huge leap in our online presence this last year and it's because of our Marketing Director, Liv Windorf, and our PR & Advertising Manager, Celeste Reyes. They are constantly coming up with new ways to expand our reach and really engage with our followers and I am so thankful they share the same passion that I do for what we're creating.

If you're reading this book, you have most likely participated in one of our epic challenges and have had the opportunity to work with one of our fabulous coaches. These women not only coach challengers, but they also find the best fit for them within our Goal Digger programs afterwards. In addition, they are all Accountability Coaches in 6 Figure Breakthrough Business Academy and Ignited Life Coaching. Their commitment and dedication allow us to really serve in a massive way.

Aleshia Wisch is one of those people that will constantly surprise you because she'll set some crazy goal and she'll make it happen. She cares about others so selflessly and has always loved this brand more than just about anybody I know. Her loyalty makes me smile.

Chaitali Desai was actually a student in 6 Figure Breakthrough when I really got to know her and I soon discovered how gifted she was. She is graceful, calm, and speaks with so much intention it always means something. She has brought such a unique element to the table with her experience around mindset and spiritual teachings. I learn from her every day.

Kathy Caviness was first a client, then a best friend, and then joined us here at Goal Digger Headquarters. She has this natural likeability and you just want to be around her. She makes everyone around her feel seen. She is constantly tapping into new sides of herself and learning how to get better and better. It's inspiring.

Vanette Grover was our first coach and, on a whim, I asked her if she wanted to help me out when we launched The Academy. That grew and grew and now she is such an integral part of how we can best serve our students and equip them to be truly aligned with the values we hold as a company. She is my voice of reason and a natural leader to all of us.

And last, but definitely not least, to all my Goal Diggers out there...You are the reason I jump out of bed in the morning, excited to get to work, and also the reason I probably stay up too late at night. You inspire me to do better, be better, and bring more to the table to help you become your best self. I truly believe we can elevate this industry together, and it all starts with bossing it up, babe.

XO,
Kimberly

INTRODUCTION

"A true diva is graceful, and talented, and strong, and fearless and brave and someone with humility."

~ Beyoncé Knowles-Carter

What does it mean to "BOSS It Up" exactly? Well, let me take you on a little trip down memory lane. Before the 1960s, women were not allowed to have a bank account. I want you to pause and think about that for a minute. It wasn't until 1974 that women were issued credit cards without a husband having to be on the account.

Now before you write this off as a book about feminism, I want to redefine all of that. I want us to not only take back our inherent power that got lost along the way, but I want us to also tap into the fiercely beautiful side of us that is the very definition of being a woman.

We are fierce and we are fabulous.

And the best way to execute this amazing combination of God-given divinity is to BOSS up in all areas of life. We must conquer our mindset, 10x our self confidence, and go out there and build the business of our dreams. .

God put us each on this earth for a reason, for a purpose greater than ourselves. I know you know it deep down in your heart. It's that stirring that keeps you up late at night. It's the daydreaming you catch yourself in when you should be focused on what's in front of you. It's the knowing that you are here to make a difference, for you, your family, and those you desire to impact.

As someone who went from being severely depressed, stuck in massive debt, struggling with alcohol addiction, to overcoming all of that and literally transforming every area of my life, I am excited to take you on this journey to truly boss up your life but also get into the specifics of how you can boss up your business and really crush your goals.

In 2017, I knew what I was doing wasn't working. I was repeating the same destructive cycle of behavior over and over again, obviously getting the same results. I knew I wanted to work from home and quit my job. I knew I wanted to get us out of debt so we could go on vacations or put our girls in sports. But what I was doing was definitely not working.

That summer, I hired Michelle Thompson to rewire my brain. I know that sounds crazy but one of my best friends, Raime Spence, said Michelle had taught her how to change her thoughts about herself when she was getting out of her depression. That got my attention.

Michelle has a very specialized approach she developed, but through my work with her I was able to reprogram my thoughts about myself from very negative to very positive. Instead of waking up telling myself I sucked and I was a bad mom, I would wake up and say, "You're gonna rock today! Get up, it's going to be awesome!"

After working with Michelle for six weeks, I was strong enough to put down the glasses (and bottles) of wine for good. This is when everything truly started transforming for me, because addiction is synonymous with destructive, right?

I was now mentally strong enough to really start working on my business. I had dabbled in network marketing for about six months and was finally ready to really grow it. I heard about social media, and after watching a few webinars, I realized this was it. This was how I was going to do it. This was how I was going to get out of debt and be able to stay home with my babies, who were one and two at the time.

The only problem was, I wasn't on social media. Dang it, it sounded like such a great idea! But then I looked at myself in the mirror and said, "Look at what you've done already. You can do anything. You can learn anything. Now go do it."

It was go-time. This was my big chance.

I enrolled in coaching programs, listened to podcasts, spent every little second I had outside of working, commuting and changing diapers to soak up anything I could get my hands on.

And I implemented.

As soon as I heard something, I would go do it. Make your Facebook™ profile inviting. Check. Post valuable content and share stuff about yourself every day. Check. Go live. Check. And on and on.

I didn't know what the heck I was doing, but I was coachable, hungry, and driven. I wanted this so bad it was all I could think about. When setbacks would occur, I would cry for about 10 minutes and then get myself back in the game. I had to or else I would never get the momentum I needed to build my business online.

In the fall of 2017, I started going live every single week, and then shortly after started my first Facebook™ Group. I told my very small audience I would coach them for free for a month and help them hit their goals. With a background in nutrition and personal training, this was a natural place for me to start.

They loved it so much they were soon asking me business questions like; How do you go live? How do you do vision boards? How do you manage your time?

Now the interesting thing is, and I want you to really hear this part, I didn't know what I was doing. I wasn't making six figures yet. I wasn't at the top of my company. We were still digging our way out of debt. But I showed up, shared what I was learning, and I cared. I answered every single comment and Facebook™ message, and went above and beyond to help anyone in my space.

Not too long after that, I held my first paid workshop and charged a whopping $15 each. I had 30 students and couldn't believe I just made that on a Saturday morning all while having a blast the entire time! I was hooked. This was my calling.

I launched The Goal Digger Girl in the spring of 2018, and we hit six figures in 90 days. I eventually got to the top of my company and am still actively in the trenches so that my teachings can be timely and relevant.

Since then, we've built our monthly reach to over 1.5 million people across all social channels, released several books, two being #1 best-seller on Amazon, have a top 50 rated podcast in the marketing sector, passed $2.5 million in revenue, and have had over 3,000 students go through our programs.

When it comes to bossing up your personal brand online, I want you to remember that this is all about learning how to show up online in a genuine and authentic way. You must know you are amazing and have value to offer. If you don't believe that, your audience will sense that.

This is about finding your voice. It's about getting dialed in to who you want to be online and who you want to serve. Once you find this sweet spot, not only will your business flourish, but so will your joy of being an entrepreneur. First, we need to light the fire within, then be the light to others, then pass on the torch.

This is me beginning that process with you.

The fire is within you, so let's BOSS It Up, Babe!

CHAPTER 1

Becoming *HER*

"Start with the end in mind. If you want to be a millionaire, talk like one, act like one, work like one."

~ Bob Proctor

Why Your Mindset Predicts Your Success

I may know what you're thinking right now and that is something along the lines of, *"Kimberly, I thought I was going to learn how to crush my business, why are we starting with this woo woo stuff?"* Admit it – I'm pretty close, aren't I?

When I look back at all my experiences in the last twenty years as a serial entrepreneur, I can tell you without a doubt, my success didn't come until I worked on my mindset. Ask anyone who is making six or seven figures, they will tell you the same thing.

It may not be the sexy marketing stuff, but it is *just* as important, if not more important, in my opinion.

So how does your mindset predict your success?

Well, you can do all of the work, show up on social media, talk to people, even send out a few emails, but if you don't believe in yourself and the value that you bring, your insecurity will be sensed by others or you will self-sabotage your success. Grab the book *The Big Leap* by Gay Hendricks if you suspect this has been happening to you because it will help you get through the barriers you put on yourself subconsciously.

As you work on building your online business, you will wonder if you are worthy of having success or if people will even want what you have to offer. I know this because I have been there. You have to have a rock-solid mindset to know that you have valuable content that can really help people and believe that you are capable of delivering.

Being an entrepreneur is like climbing a mountain. There are highs and lows, peaks and valleys. You will get a win (*i.e.: new client, awesome teammate, etc.*) and feel on top of the world. Then, before you know it, someone quits, you get an online troll hating on you, or you get in a fight with your husband.

You will want to quit.

This is when the warrior mind we are about to cultivate comes into play. When these setbacks occur, you will look them in the eye and give them a wink, *"Try me"* you will whisper, because you know you are truly unstoppable. You have worked too hard and come too far to allow outside circumstances to dictate how you will respond.

When I was still at a job I hated and only making a few thousand a month from my side hustle, I imagined what it would be like to work from home running an online empire.

How would I dress?

How would I speak to others?

What would I be doing throughout the day?

Who would I get to work with?

When I did this exercise, I would close my eyes, envision it, and smile knowing it was on the way.

I had to ignore what was in front of me to change my circumstances.

I had to tell myself that I was a six-figure earner and *feel* like I really was. It took less than six months for me to make that a reality and I can tell you that *this* daily practice was a huge part of that.

What thoughts do you need to let go of that are not serving you? Are there certain behaviors or habits you have that are not supporting a six or seven figure mindset?

_____

_____

_____

_____

_____

_____

_____

_____

_____

_____

_____

_____

_____

_____

_____

_____

_____

_____

_____

_____

_____

_____

_____

_____

_____

_____

_____

_____

Addressing Blocks & Smashing Them

As you can probably tell, I'm not one to dwell on the past, but who you are today is a collection of all the beliefs and programming that have been implanted on you since you were born.

I've heard some experts say that the majority of our beliefs are developed by the time we enter first grade. That is freaking crazy if you really think about it.

And we just go on with our lives into adulthood, never questioning those beliefs, and by the time we become conscious enough to change them, they are so strongly rooted that they are literally *automatic*, and very deep into our subconscious minds.

I was reading about a little girl who used to sing all the time, like most little girls like to do. Her mother was raising her alone, so she was working ridiculous hours to make ends meet. After a long day of work, totally spent, her mother yelled at her to shut up and that her singing was giving her a headache.

At four years old, the little girl decided right then and there that her singing was ugly and never sang another note again. It wasn't until adulthood, after intense therapy, that she realized where her mother was coming from and discovered she had a beautiful voice and began a singing career.

Beliefs are everything.

The good news is any belief can be changed. It does take awareness, intention, and a whole lot of repetition but it does work. And once you make the time commitment to change them, the benefits can last a lifetime.

The influential people in our lives have the most impact on what we believe about ourselves. Most commonly are our parents, grandparents, siblings, teachers, bosses, coaches, and our peers.

Again, those that you were around the most through the age of seven have the biggest impact on our beliefs about ourselves. Reflecting on those people would be a good place to start as you identify beliefs passed onto you about yourself or the world. We'll take them one by one to replace them if they are no longer serving you.

When I first started going through this work with my life coach when I was 20, I felt a lot of anger towards my parents. I was tempted to call them up and let them know *exactly* how I felt. However, I would recommend working through your limiting beliefs and leaving it at that. If you want to take it further, I would consult with a professional.

Our number one priority is to improve your relationship with yourself, and secondly is your relationships with others. You'll see as we go along you may no longer feel the need to even address it.

Remember this in the meantime – your parents inherited their belief system and programming from their parents and so on. It is so ingrained that most of the time they don't even realize how they're negatively impacting others and just think it's normal.

But *you* are enlightened. *You* are taking control of your life.

You are different. Most everyone else just goes through life doing the same thing their parents did and then passes it onto the next generation. Letting go of any resentment you feel towards anyone influential in your life is very healing and freeing. It's not easy, but it is better for your overall well-being and happiness.

To set you free from the past, we are going to make a list of old beliefs that are potentially holding you back or causing self-sabotage known as *"upper limits."* In Gay Hendricks' book I mentioned earlier, *The Big Leap,* he explains that upper limits are basically old belief systems that tend to hold us back from growing or reaching new successes in our lives if we don't acknowledge them and work through reframing them.

This is especially true when it comes to our association with making money because it is so deeply rooted in our family and society. If you grew up hearing, "*Money doesn't grow on trees*," you know exactly what I'm talking about.

And to show you how hidden these limiting beliefs are, I'll share something with you that I discovered about myself as my income greatly increased over the last couple of years.

I noticed that whenever someone would come to our house, such as a handyman, and I had to take them through the house and out back by the pool and outdoor kitchen area, I would get really embarrassed. We have an acre of land and live in the hill country, so the view is really nice. The same feeling would come up whenever I was around other people in my brand-new Lexus, that I paid cash for when I bought it. Embarrassment.

When I talked to my coach, she asked me why. I started crying because I realized I thought those people would think that I didn't earn those nice things, but that I was a housewife and my husband made all the money. (*Side note: no judgment for you SAHMs, but work has always been a strong part of my identity, so this was a trigger for me*).

Where was all of this coming from? My limiting beliefs in full force! I had grown up on reduced lunch and layaway. We literally didn't have enough money for me to eat food like normal kids or have new clothes for school.

I grew up in lack. So when you suddenly are hit with abundance in a short period of time, your subconscious is not buying it.

This is just my example with money, but we can also sabotage relationships with someone really great or isolate new friendships because of old, crappy beliefs we are still carrying around from childhood.

To help you get started at identifying and reframing your old beliefs, I've picked a few of the most common areas to look at, but obviously you'll know what you need to work on most. In the left column, write out your old belief and in the right column create your new belief statement.

Categories:
- Self-Worth
- Money
- Self-Image
- Intelligence

- Time
- Ability
- Health
- Family
- Influence/Leadership
- Running a Business

Example:

Old Belief

New Belief

I am not worthy. I am not   I   am   more   than   enough.

    good enough.   I am special.

List any and all that you can think of here:

Old Belief

New Belief

_____   _____

_____   _____

_____   _____

_____   _____

_____   _____

_____   _____

_____   _____

_____   _____

_____   _____

_____   _____

_____   _____

_____   _____

_____   _____

_____   _____

_____   _____

_____   _____

_____   _____

_____   _____

_____   _____

Getting Big Girl Boss Goals

I recently learned the billionaire Warren Buffet's strategy for goal setting and fell in love with its simplicity. We'll talk about implementation next but for now, follow his easy three-step strategy for goal setting.

Step 1

List out 25 career goals you would like to achieve in your lifetime:

1. _____

_____

2. _____

_____

3. _____

_____

4. _____

_____

5. _____

_____

6. _____

_____

7. _____

_____

8. _____

_____

9. _____

_____

10. _____

_____

11. _____

_____

12. _____

_____

13. _____

_____

14. _____

_____

15. _____

_____

16. _____

_____

17. _____

_____

18. _____

_____

19. _____

_____

20. _____

_____

21. _____

_____

22. _____

_____

23. _____

_____

24. _____

_____

25. _____

_____

Step 2

From step one, circle the top five you would like to work on first and write them here:

1. _____

_____

2. _____

_____

3. _____

_____

4. _____

_____

5. _____

_____

Step 3

Focus on *only* those five and do everything you can to avoid the rest (*aka: don't get distracted*).

And that's it! I would recommend creating a vision board or a vision movie of you implementing these five goals and review them frequently. You can find my Vision Board

Workshop inside Goal Digger University if you would like more guidance.

The L.I.T. Model
In the corporate world, you are paid to do certain tasks, ranging from big to small. You just do it, or you won't have a job for very long. But as an entrepreneur, we are a volunteer army.

We are our own boss.

No one is telling us what to do or "motivating us."

We have to do it.
That is the biggest challenge when it comes to having success in your business, outside of mindset, that you will face.

Education constipation is a real thing and fake working is an epidemic amongst us. And that's where the L.I.T. model came to be.

L.I.T. stands for Learn, Implement, Take Action. Pretty much everyone has the L down, as the knowledge of what you need to grow your business is readily shared across social media, in books, and on podcasts.

The I, Implement, is where a lot of the frustration and procrastination sets in. Without implementation, we don't feel good about our work and have that nagging feeling we aren't doing enough. So, as soon as you learn something, your job is to implement it as fast as possible.

One thing I'll share that has really served me is to put deadlines in place that will force me to learn it. For example, the very first 15-minute Facebook™ party I hosted, I had no idea what the posts were going to be in the group, what content was going to be covered in the Facebook™ Live or what the giveaway looked like. But I scheduled it...and guess what? I figured it out!

And, finally, T is to Take Action. Every single day you need to take action to move forward in your business. For you, it might be following up with leads, connecting with new prospects on social media, or doing that video you said you were going to do. Either way, you need to be working on your business every day.

You've probably heard these daily actions called IPAs (*Income Producing Activities*) and you will often hear me refer to them as Money Making Activities.

It's not enough to have a clean office space or a cute logo on your website. You need to take action.

In my opinion, you need to take massive, imperfect action, every single day.

Imagine what your business would look like in one year if you did *that*?

Mastering Manifestation

Manifesting is simply the act of placing your desires in your mind's eye and then following inspired action to make them a reality. Inspired action takes your desires and pairs them up with the Universe giving you clues as ways to bring them to fruition. It's that little nudge from your inner voice giving you an idea, a great feeling, or some magical coincidence that makes you shake your head in awe.

You know what I'm talking about.

The secret is to act on it as soon as humanly possible and not let doubt creep in. For example, if you think of a great idea for a Facebook™ Live topic or a prospect pops into your head you hadn't thought to reach out to previously, then you need to follow through as soon as you can.

Acknowledge any negative thoughts or limiting beliefs for what they are and push through. You will get stronger and stronger as you act on this inspiration and grow more confident.

That's literally my business plan!

All I do is follow inspired action. I know it sounds crazy but I legit do not have any long-term specific plans because everything is intuitive for me.

When I released *The Goal Digger* in the fall of 2018, I took the girls to visit my mom for a couple of weeks and got back on a Saturday. The very next day, that internal voice said, *"You need to launch the mastermind you've been toying around with in your head. All of your followers say they wish you were their upline, do this for them. Oh, and you need to launch it by October 1st."*

October 1st was that Friday! There was *no way* I was going to be able to figure out the format, the content, promote it to my audience, *and* get the membership fees set up to run monthly...it just wasn't going to be possible.

That Friday, October 1st, The Goal Digger Mastermind was launched and we had well over 100 members register.

If you obey, and listen to that little voice, it *always* works out.

Fear vs. Faith-Based Thinking

Action is all about decision making. We make decisions all day long. Thousands and thousands of them actually. Your life is a collection of the decisions you make repeatedly on a daily basis.

So, to make a shift and move in the direction you want in your life, I encourage you to make faith-based decisions versus ones made from fear.

I always ask myself, *"Am I making this decision out of fear or acting on faith?"*

It really does work and keeps you in check to make sure you're not allowing your ego to take the driver's seat. I've made some scary decisions in my career but they've all worked out beautifully because they were based on faith. Give it a try!

How to Become a Powerful Manifestor

I'm sure you've heard me say, *"I totally manifested that."* And you may be wondering, what the heck is she talking about, right? Basically, another way to describe manifesting is claiming something will come forth into existence in your world.

There's a bit more of an energetic quality to it versus just setting a goal.

You can literally manifest anything.

And the neat thing is, your job isn't to figure out how it is going to happen. You just have to be clear on how it will make you feel to have it become a reality in your life and do your best to match up vibrationally to it.

We'll cover some different techniques next on how you can manifest things into your life sooner than later. One thing to note is that you can't go looking for what you manifested all the time because then you're focusing on *not* having it and therefore causing it to not materialize.

I know that's a bit tricky, but you almost need to pretend it has already happened and "feel" what it would feel like to have it be real. The more often you can be in that place, the sooner it will come into existence.

It's pretty surreal when you manifest something you never thought possible. Of course, you can start small, such as trying to manifest loose change to appear in random places, then grow it from there.

For one year, I imagined what it would be like to work from home. To sit in front of my cell phone or webcam, doing Facebook™ Lives or teaching someone something via Zoom. You know I love to talk! I could see myself creating, teaching, and inspiring. I would take myself to that pretend place so often that sometimes I thought it was real.

Today, I sit at my desk and all those things I imagined for so long are my reality now. It didn't come suddenly for me because I played the scene over and over in my mind so often it had become as natural as breathing.

The trick is to get into that feel good place and make your subconscious believe it is already here. Then the Universe will get to work and give you the opportunities to take action and bring it into existence.

Meditation

When most of us think of meditation, we conjure up images from the movie *Eat, Pray, Love* when the author Elizabeth Gilbert made her way to India and spent hours upon hours in silence meditating dutifully among others. However, with this misguided interpretation of what it is, we miss out on what it *can* be.

Meditation is the gateway to extreme mental focus and peak productivity for all entrepreneurs.

When I do private coaching with my clients, just like most entrepreneurs, they have tons of ideas, loads of goals, and big dreams. However, when we dig in deep to look at their daily activity, focused action and productivity are almost always non-existent.

It's the catch-22 for most wanting the laptop lifestyle. Making the commitment to daily meditation practices can be the best thing they can do to get what they want.

Entrepreneurs are extremely creative and because of that, our minds tend to go in a million different directions all the time, and it can be super hard to focus. When we set out to tackle our day, we tend to feel disorganized.

To gain mental clarity and efficiency with the projects in front of us, meditation can help us get there. By quieting the mind, even for a short bit, it allows the brain to be trained to focus for longer periods of time.

Just like we do strength training in the gym to increase muscle endurance, we can "strength train" our mind by incorporating daily meditation. People often quit the gym after the first few times of attending because it's hard or doesn't come easy yet.

It's the same thing with meditation. It takes time to build the muscle that allows you to develop laser-like focus and be able to cultivate peak productivity daily.

It's ideal to start your day off with meditation but I personally will do it as soon as I can find a quiet space or a break in my schedule to do so. I encourage you to try the app, Headspace, and do the daily challenge of starting with five or ten minutes in length to develop the habit.

Studies have shown even just ten minutes a day can improve the neural pathways in your brain in only two weeks' time!

So, what are you waiting for? It's time to meditate :).

My daily meditation goal is _____ minutes.

Your Miracle Morning to Crush Your Day

Play around with the different mindset techniques I shared with you to see what you found to be the most beneficial. What you need can ebb and flow as you go along, but I encourage you to narrow the different options down and craft your miracle morning.

Have you ever heard the phrase, *"Win the morning, win the day?"* This is so true!

This is where you decide what your non-negotiables are each and every morning.

No matter how busy your day is going to be, you are committed to getting up early enough to make it happen.

I remember one of the turning points for me was when I got up at 4:45 am every morning so I would have time to get ready for work, do my miracle morning, and then get the girls up and ready for the day.

Yes, it takes discipline. Yes, the snooze button is going to have your name written all over it. But if you are consistent and stick with it, it *will* transform your life.

How can it not?

So go ahead and write down what you will do during your miracle morning. Here are some ideas to get you started:

- Meditate
- Pray
- Tap (also known as EFT)
- List out powerful words of affirmation
- Review your goals and write them in present tense
- Write down what you're grateful for
- Journal your thoughts and feelings
- Read a devotional
- Do a guided visualization from YouTube
- Look at or watch your Vision Board/Movie

My Miracle Morning Routine:

_____

_____

_____

_____

_____

_____

_____

_____

_____

_____

_____

_____

_____

_____

_____

_____

_____

_____

_____

_____

Your CEO Space

Because disorganization and overwhelm are such a common struggle amongst budding entrepreneurs like yourself, I want to address your workspace. If you are setting up shop on some janky card table in the middle of your busy living room, I am going to challenge you on this.

I am all about working with what you have but if you want to become a 6 or 7 figure earner, you need to start acting like one.

Is your space organized?

Does it make you feel good when you sit down in your chair and get to work?

Do you have all of the tools you need (*i.e.: a working computer*) to really crush your productivity and be efficient?

If not, you need to carve out time within the next seven days to clean up your area or find a place for you to work. There are co-working spaces these days that are extremely affordable if your home is not going to cut it.

Do what you can with what you have for now but I want you to constantly ask yourself, "Do I have everything I need for the better version of myself I am currently creating?"

CHAPTER 2

Girl Boss Daily Domination

"Time isn't the main thing. It's the only thing."

~ Miles Davis

Set Your DMO in Stone

The #1 difference I've noticed between those that are growing their business the way that they want to and are feeling satisfied with their daily productivity versus those that aren't is how they spend their time.

Those that plan ahead and have control of their schedule win. Even if you must have a fluid schedule, you can still take control and plan out your day.

With your goals in front of you, take time each Sunday evening or Monday morning to map out your week. Time block everything down to 15-minute increments.

Even if you have to move items around on a whim, you at least should have them down so that they can be rescheduled. Take a look and make sure the very important things are showing up in your calendar. Is there time to do your mindset work? Exercise? Work on your biz?

Next, utilize *The Goal Digger's DMO: Hour of Power* worksheet found in the book resources section at **thegoaldiggergirl.com/bossitup**. Ideally, this is completed first before you work on any of your other items on your to-do list.

Now, before you tell yourself you don't have an hour a day to do this, I need to call you out on that. I am saying this out of love, but if you can't take 30-60 minutes a day to work on your mindset, develop your skills, and take action in your business, you may want to readjust your priorities.

When I first started my Hour of Power, I did 15 minutes in the morning, which included my mindset work and posting on social media.

Midday, I would hop back online and eat lunch at my desk. I never left my office at work that first year into my online business. I was obsessed. During this session, I would do all of my MMAs (Money Making Activities) such as reach outs, follow ups, and asking prospects to take a look at what I had to offer. I knew if I waited until nighttime to do it, it may just not happen. Sound familiar?

After the girls were in bed and I spent a little time with Scott, I would head to my home office and get to work. This is where I would watch a training or maybe do a Facebook™ Live. It was the stuff I enjoyed more because I was exhausted at this point and knew I wouldn't have the motivation to do anything else.

But listen, and this is key, THIS is what worked for ME. You cannot adopt my workflow and expect it to work perfectly for you. Only you know when you are most energetic or when you have space open up in your day. One of my best friends still has her youngest at home so she does her entire Hour of Power during her midday nap. Find what works for you.

You may need to sacrifice some sleep for a short period of time until you get a system and become efficient. You may have to give up some of your favorite shows. It just comes down to your commitment and how bad you want this. Check out *The Miracle Morning for Network Marketers* to hear success stories on how others made it happen.

Test Drive the Car from Point A to B

To wrap up the L.I.T. module, we are going to get crystal clear on where you're at and where you'd like to be. You've already determined what your priorities are, so have that in the forefront as you decide what you'd like to see in your life. Setting goals is an amazing habit but sometimes I feel as if the emotional connection is missing. Try this method as well.

Taking the different areas of your life, I want you to complete the following statements replacing business with the appropriate topic:

The way I'd describe my <u>business</u> currently is…

_____

_____

_____

_____

_____

_____

The way I'd like to see my <u>business</u> is…

_____

_____

_____

_____

_____

_____

One thing I can do to get aligned is…

_____

_____

_____

_____

_____

_____

For the last statement, I want you to think of ways you can "*feel*" what it would be like to have that goal achieved and a reality in your life.

Could you take a day off of work and "*work from home*" running your amazingly successful business?

Could you go test drive that brand new Lexus and get a selfie while you're at it?

Yes, yes, and yes!

Delegating

Oh my word! When I think back to the hours upon hours I spent mailing out samples to prospects, I want to cringe. It made sense to do it myself when I started out, but once my business started growing, it would have made more sense to find someone else who could do it for me. Do you have a teenager or a friend who would love to help you out part-time? Trading products for services is one of the best old school ways to get some help on your side without breaking the bank.

To determine if you should delegate the activity or do it yourself, the first question is to ask: Is this a Money Making Activity? If yes, you should be doing it. That is the number one priority of your business and you need to have your hands in it.

If it isn't, then you can determine what your estimated worth is per hour and decide if it makes more sense for you to do it or contract someone else to do it.

Saying No

I know it's super cliché, but honestly, if you really want to make entrepreneurship a career or reach six figures and beyond, you have to get really good at saying no. You need to say no to invitations, commitments, online distractions, Netflix, *Real Housewives*, etc.

I know that sounds extreme, and I get it, but I'm not asking you to do it forever.

A lot of times newbie entrepreneurs get frustrated because they're not seeing the progress in their business that they'd hoped for. But what they don't realize is that often they're working their business way less than they need to in order to make their dreams a reality.

Start with saying no to the things that eat away at your productivity the most and go from there.

Dial it Down for Peak Productivity

Now we are going to take your DMO and dial it down so you know *exactly* what activity you should be doing every day to grow your business strategically. I remember when I was starting out and saw others having rapid success and I thought if I could just figure out what they were *actually* doing every day, I would go do it. It seemed like such a mystery.

So, think of your DMO as the birdseye view of your day in regards to working on it and this section will be breaking each area down into specifics. I'm only going to focus on the business growth piece, you can decide what your specific mindset work looks like, etc.

Because entrepreneurs are squirrely by nature, having a checklist to follow is going to keep you on track and get you hyper focused.

Doesn't that sound awesome?

You can find the Daily Activity Tracker in the book resources section **thegoaldiggergirl.com/bossitup**.

When you first start out, this will feel like a lot and your mind will probably come up with seemingly legit reasons not to finish it.

However, for those that are committed and stick with it, not only do they feel in control of their business for the first time ever, they also get amazing results.

Are you committed?

Daily Activity Tracker

Morning	Monday	Tuesday	Wednesday	Thursday	Friday	Saturday	Sunday
Post on Facebook (personal/groups)							
Post on Facebook Stories							
Post on Instagram and in IG Stories/Check Comments							
Check Messenger/Message Prospects							
Check Notifications							
Comment on People's Posts who Comment on My Posts							
Add 10 New Friends (delete as needed)							
Send Happy Birthday Messages							
Comment on 10 Posts from See 1st Friends							
Mid-Day							
Post on Facebook (personal/groups)							
Post in Facebook and Instagram Stories							
Check Messenger/Message Prospects							
Evening							
Facebook Live 1-2 times Weekly (personal/groups)							
Check Messenger/Message Prospects							
Check Notifications							
Comment on People's Posts who Comment on My Posts							
Add 10 New Friends (delete as needed)							
Add Value to 1-3 Private Groups (ie: NM Moms)							
Follow Ups							
Daily Totals:							
# of New Exposures (product or business opportunity)							
# of New Customers							
# of New Business Builders							
Weekly Total:							

Types of Posts: inspiring, empowering, personal share, product post, biz post, entertaining, educational/tips, lives

Tracking Your Prospects like a BOSS

We are going to spend an entire chapter on lead generation and closing, but, we are going to get a jump on tracking prospects now, so you can start by adding your leads to Trello or a CRM.

I want you to start fresh with adding names if you are feeling as if you haven't been great at this and don't have them easily accessible.

Basically your job is to move names through your sales funnel.

Every day.

Rinse and repeat my friend.

I know it sounds so easy but guess what? 95% of online marketers don't do this! Lucky for us, you are in the 5% that do. So, have your tracker open every day and keep it updated.

This is your book of business.

This is your future earnings.

This is your sanity.

Once you have gotten to the point in conversation where you have shared what you do with your prospect and asked them if you could get them more info (*insert appropriate example*), then you move them to the exposed list.

You know, of course, to send them some kind of 3rd party tool for duplication purposes and social proof, so that's your next step.

Then, get them into a three way chat with your upline or someone who can be in that messenger convo with your prospect. Don't wait for them to take action on the 3rd party tool, just go right into the chat.

From there, you either have a new customer, team member, client or someone to follow up with.

And that is literally your sales cycle. Throw in some referrals as you go and boom – you are rockin' and rolling!

Take Control with Time Blocking
I'm going to teach you how to implement time blocking, get organized, and get laser-focused on the task at hand.

How would it feel to end your day *knowing* you'd set your project list for the day and implemented most of it, if not all of it?

When we have unstructured time, we get nothing done. Freshman year of college comes to mind, ha!

I remember when I was on maternity leave with Elise; it was night and day compared to Addison. With her, I was finishing my PhDs so I was under constant deadlines and therefore uber-productive.

With Elise, I was unemployed so I didn't have anything demanding my attention outside of my brand new wiggly baby who had the appetite of a teenage football player.

Each day I could see Scott coming into the main entrance of our neighborhood because we live high up on a hill. I would put Elise in the baby swing and speed around the house like the Tasmanian devil.

I'd quickly change out of my PJs, brush my teeth and throw a little mascara on. Every single day I would wonder what the heck I did, even though I felt "busy" all day.

Have you ever felt this way?

Sometimes one of my followers will message me saying they are working 10-12 hours a day but not making any progress in their business. I'll have them do a 15-minute time blocking challenge to identify how much is really spent on MMAs and how much is fake working.

I'm continually shocked at how many don't get back to me.

The truth doesn't hurt if it sets you free.

So are you ready to conquer your calendar?!

I heard an interesting statistic from an expert on productivity and it is worth sharing. When you are in the middle of a task, get interrupted, and you stop to handle it (*ie: answer the front door*), it can take up to 23 minutes to fully get back into the task at hand!

I just read an article from the *Washington Post* that said the average employee gets interrupted every three minutes and five seconds.

\#MindBlown.

Now let's say you are below average and only get interrupted 20 times in a six-hour period, that is still potentially six hours of lost productivity!

What the focus, right?

Just like you, my back was up against the wall trying to find time to build my business on top of my full-time job and family. When I, not only, learned time blocking but actually became disciplined enough to implement it, my life completely transformed.

And I kinda became obsessed with it.

I first learned time blocking when I took on a freelance job writing articles for YogaLifestyles.com. I repeatedly found myself up at 1 am twice a month when the article was due and it was so stressful I started resenting something I had previously enjoyed.

My therapist, Michelle Thompson (*aka my miracle worker*), asked me if I had any down time at work such as a lunch break to be able to knock the articles out. I realized that Monday afternoons before our weekly management meetings were always quiet and I could do it then.

It took a couple of tries to stick with it but I can't even describe to you how amazing it felt to have the articles done *before* they were due! I have always been a just-in-time-delivery kinda girl since high school so I really knocked my socks off with this new behavior.

I felt in control for the first time since becoming a mother.

And I want that for you too so let's dive in!

Before we set up your master calendar, I want to share an analogy I've heard from other time management experts that will help you see how this works.

Remember back in school when you received your class schedule and you'd run through the flow of the day? You'd assess when you would go back to your locker for which books and where the next class would be?

You'd get to science class, take out your science book and only focus on that subject matter. You wouldn't pull out your art project in science class and start working on that, correct? If you did, your teacher and classmates would look at you in horror and you wouldn't be able to blame them.

When the bell would ring, you'd pack up your science books, head to art class and pull out the appropriate materials for that subject matter and only focus on art at that time. Let me ask you a question: how productive were you?

Well we're going to do the same thing with your schedule but with topics such as family, exercise, prospecting, social media, etc. Now, you won't physically be able to go to different classrooms to distinctively switch gears so what I like to do is pretend I'm putting a different hat on to indicate a different role I'm fulfilling. This is #EntrepreneurLife in a nutshell.

For example, there are many times in the late afternoon when Scott will come home unexpectedly with the girls. I literally can be in the middle of an email and they'll come barreling into my office all excited from their busy school days and wanting to share all the juicy details with me. Once I hear the garage door open, I imagine myself swapping out my Goal Digger hat for my very broken-in Mom hat.

It totally works.

Creating Habits that Stick

In order to make these strategies work for you long term, you need to create habits that stick. Just like with dieting or starting a new exercise program, you can survive off of the initial motivation to get started. This is why so many people quit after a few days or weeks. They have that bad day and give in to their old ways and before you know it, they've quit altogether.

The key is to work at it every single day. Because if you miss one day, you miss two and then...you get the point.

Think about other things you've started in the past. Why did you stop them?

Have you ever rediscovered something awesome that you were doing before and wondered, *"Why did I stop this before? It was really working for me!"* It's because, at some point, you thought to skip it for just one day and then you did it again and fell right out of the habit.

So, to create lasting changes, you *have* to do your mindset work every day. Even if you're on vacation or sick in the hospital. You may be thinking *no way*, but if it's important to you, you will find the time.

One time we went to the Dominican Republic and I was still breast pumping. We'd booked the trip so far out I didn't even think about that being an issue. Well, four times a day, I had to go into the hotel room and pump. Not the most glamorous trip ever but I did stick with it because my baby depended on it. Your dreams are as important as that little baby of mine!

Act like it and stay committed. Okay?

It can be helpful to have some kind of accountability partner to check in with so feel free to pair up with another Goal Digger who is working on crushing her business too.

Staying on track just means staying intentional and focused. It really is the most important thing you can do.

CHAPTER 3

Hey, Babe!

"If people like you they will listen to you, but if they trust you, they'll do business with you."

~ Zig Ziglar

Who She Is

One of the biggest mistakes that online marketers make is thinking because their product or service is for everyone...then they should market to everyone, right?

Wrong.

This is referred to as broad marketing and throughout this chapter, you are going to learn how to stop throwing stuff out on social media hoping the right people come to you to learn more about what you have to offer.

When you get clear with your messaging, who you're serving, and the problems you are solving, it will become very clear to your ideal avatar that you are the obvious choice.

Wouldn't it be nice to stop convincing and have your prospects actually wanting to work with you or buy from you?

In addition, another common pitfall is to cater to the types of customers or clients you're already getting instead of deciding who you want to work with.

For example, if you're constantly getting the money objection, you need to focus on attracting those who have more money. Those people can easily afford what you have and/or they see the value in what you're offering and are willing to spend the money.

Let the scarcity mindset go and embrace an abundant mindset. There are billions of people on social media, you just need to find the ones in your space, and this will allow you to free up your energy and focus on those that truly matter.

To determine who your ideal avatar is, answer the following questions thinking about the type of person you want to attract, not who you necessarily are serving currently.

What type of experiences has your ideal avatar had that shaped who they are today?

_____

_____

_____

_____

_____

_____

What is important to her when it comes to money and why? (*i.e.: value, a deal, high quality, etc.*)

_____

_____

_____

_____

_____

_____

What is her "why" and how does this drive her behavior?

_____

_____

_____

_____

_____

_____

Are there any things that she may be avoiding or are blocks
for her? (*i.e.: lack of time, etc.*)

_____

_____

_____

_____

_____

_____

What is her mindset like and confidence level?

_____

_____

_____

_____

_____

What is her vision for herself and those closest in her life
long term?

_____

_____

_____

_____

_____

_____

Jot down any potential fears, objections, prior negative experiences, etc. that may be holding her back from working with you:

_____

_____

_____

_____

_____

_____

What season of life is your ideal avatar in? (*ie: raising young kids, entering retirement, etc.*) What will you need to be considerate of?

_____

_____

_____

_____

_____

_____

What is her home life like? How will this impact her readiness to buy from you or become a part of your team/program?

_____

_____

_____

_____

_____

_____

What is her daily routine like? How can you make her life better?

_____

_____

_____

_____

_____

_____

What makes her feel happy or fulfilled? How can you add to this?

_____

_____

_____

_____

_____

_____

As you can see, your ideal avatar is a very specific person. We'll get into demographics later in this section of the book but for now, jot down additional thoughts as they come up to get even clearer on who this person is and what makes her tick.

The Path to Pain Points

In your messaging and your marketing, you may be focusing on the benefits of what your product or service can do instead of solving a problem. Even if something seems really amazing to you, it means nothing to your prospect unless it's going to make her life easier or better.

As you work on your social media content, the underlying focus should always be What's In It For Them (*WIIFT*). Create curiosity addressing pain points and mention the solution you have to solve their problems.

To identify your ideal avatar's pain points, here are a couple of suggestions.

- Use AnswerThePublic.com and type in a question you think your prospect may be asking.
- Do a poll on your personal profile, in your Stories, or inside of a Facebook™ group and ask questions that will lead to pain points. For example, you could ask *"When it comes to weight loss, my biggest struggle is..."* and then have pain points for them to choose from and encourage them to comment with options you may have not listed.
- Reach out to your current customer base and ask them what their favorite benefit is so far to get clues as to what pain points you are helping with.

Complete the following worksheet and keep it handy whenever you're crafting a curiosity post, a Story or putting together content for your Facebook™ Live. Remember to do this for the product/service and the business opportunity if applicable.

Pain Point	Solution

Find Her in Facebook™ Groups

Now it's time to become a marketing detective. It's one thing to think about your Ideal Avatar on paper and quite another to see her in action!

We are going to find 2-3 groups that make sense for you to lead with the product when the opportunity arises and a couple that are business-related.

Facebook™ Group Names:

_____

_____

_____

_____

_____

_____

_____

_____

_____

The intention is to hang out in these groups and go through the following three phases to start identifying and connecting with your Ideal Avatar.

1. Observe: For this initial step, the entire goal is to get the feel for the group and determine if it will make your list of qualified groups that are worth hanging out in. Notice how often members are posting, what is the tone of the group, do you see your Ideal Avatar within the members?

2. Engage: Whenever someone posts inside of the group and you can add to the conversation, do so

without selling. You can reiterate their problem if appropriate and leave it open ended. For example, let's say someone posted that they struggle with frizzy hair in the summer humidity. You could comment that you had the same issue for years but are so thankful you found something that tamed your curls. Feel free to reach out privately in messenger but don't do anything in the feed.

3. Add Value: Once you've spent a bit of time engaging where the members start to recognize you, you can now add value. Going back to our hair example, you could post that you found five steps to fight the frizz and to comment if they want the article. That's adding value without selling. When people comment, they are warm leads! Message them privately about your products and see if they'd like more info on what helped you with your hair.

After you've spent a few days or so in each group, make a decision if it is worth your time to check into these groups each day. If it is, go ahead and add them to your Daily Activity Tracker. I, personally, have an additional column on my Prospecting Tracker that says Facebook™ Groups and I post them there so I can easily find them.

Notice how you feel when you're in the group and pick up on the tone. Is it positive, productive and beneficial to be a group member? This is an indicator that your Ideal Avatar and potential prospects are indeed inside the group.

On the flip side, a strong warning. If your nature or goal is to help people get out of bad situations, for example, someone who has no money and is about to be evicted from her home, then you will most likely be drawn to prospects like that. Yellow personalities tend to want to "help" or "save" people from their situations. And people can absolutely come out of dire situations and have the most inspiring success story of all time.

However, if you are constantly hearing that your prospects are broke and can't afford your product or get started in the business, then you are most likely not attracting your Ideal Avatar. Your Ideal Avatar can find a way to purchase your products and have the money to join your team or purchase one of your coaching packages.

Keep this in mind as you assess your Facebook™ Groups initially to determine if the feel and tone of the group truly matches your Ideal Avatar qualities.

An advanced strategy is to make friends with the moderators and admins of the Facebook™ Groups. I would take this step after you've completed the three steps above and are for sure going to move forward in spending time within the group.

Friend request the moderators and admins and send them a message such as, *"Hey there! I just wanted to tell you how much I appreciate you organizing this group and that I am getting a lot of value out of it. I love to do guest trainings so if you ever need anything, please let me know. I'm happy to help. Take care!"*

Working on finding your Ideal Avatar in Facebook™ Groups is such an effective strategy that I've seen leaders build their teams straight from them without posting much at all on their newsfeed or in their Stories. If you're in a situation where you want to be a bit more covert about your business, then prospecting in Facebook™ Groups should make the top of the list for your recruiting strategies.

Survey Your Audience

Your Ideal Avatar may end up being different than who you originally envisioned her to be while you're going through this process. There are many, many excellent clues around you already that are telling as to who she really is.

We will use feedback from your current audience to reflect on what you wrote so far to determine if you need to adjust anything. This will also give you great insights for a later chapter when we get more into personal branding.

When I moved my network marketing business to social media in the fall of 2017, everyone online knew me as "FitKim," which was my brand since 2011. I built that brand mostly in person via workshops and TV appearances, so the only online presence I had was occasionally posting on my Facebook™ Business Page.

I knew I wanted to shift to business coaching and focus on training those in online marketing, but I couldn't necessarily come in out of nowhere and start with content that was so very different from what I'd been sharing for years.

So instead, I surveyed my audience to find a way to bridge what I had been known for to the direction that I wanted to go. I asked questions to my health and wellness audience about goal setting and putting together their plan for the next year. I did polls and surveys around key attributes they saw in me that had helped them on their wellness journey.

For example, one of the needs that quickly came from my audience was learning how to plan out and master their day. They wanted to work out and meal prep but just couldn't seem to get a grip. So, I did trainings around that but also talked about how it could help with your work as well. I mentioned personal examples of me building on social media and needing to make sure I reached out to new people and followed up accordingly. I connected the dots for them because that was the direction I wanted to go.

Before you knew it, I was training on topics like social media, personal branding, Facebook™ Lives, etc. and my following was growing rapidly.

Yes, a few people didn't continue to follow me because they were not interested in learning those things and that's okay. They were not my Ideal Avatar. But all the others were and those numbers quickly grew because I was so clear on who I was serving and the content I was offering.

For you, start with your closest friends or co-workers that you trust (*ie: team members*). Ask them what they have learned the most from you and what advice they naturally go to you for above all else. You can draw correlations as you go through this. If they say they go to you when they are feeling down, you know that that is a great attribute if you want to focus on empowering women and lifting them up.

Next stop is your Facebook™ personal profile. Do a post such as "*If I had a magic wand, one thing I would improve in my life is* _____" and prompt them to fill in the sentence. You will learn so much about your current audience!

You can do a spin off of this in your Stories and use the poll feature. Keep in mind who your Ideal Avatar is and ask a question to find her. An example would be a Stories sequence sharing how you overcame some health struggles and now you are feeling amazing. Your poll could say, "*Wanna know how I did it?*" with choices such as YES or I'M CURIOUS.

For those that answer your Facebook™ post or poll, you can sift and sort and find true prospects. Connect with them to chat more. Be genuine, ask questions, and you can truly open up the door to a conversation that can go in a positive direction.

If you have a Facebook™ Group you are actively running or an email list, you can send out a survey using Google Forms, JotForm or Survey Monkey. Put together questions based on the fact finding you did at the beginning of this chapter.

Your goal is to uncover your current audience's pain points, goals, needs and desires. The exciting thing is that you will most likely uncover that your Ideal Avatar is within your current audience!

On the flip side, if you are finding a huge disconnect between your current audience and the direction you want to go, you may need to reconsider the solutions you are going to offer with your content or build a different audience.

For example, if you want to help women lose weight after having a baby and the majority of your audience are crafters who love DIY projects, you will need to focus on prospecting in Facebook™ Groups to find the women who want to lose pregnancy weight. The other option is to reposition your Ideal Avatar to moms who love running a home, wellness, crafts and other interests centered around the home.

Yes, you can eventually shift to just focusing on moms wanting to lose baby weight, but to start, get traction from your current audience so that way you have some momentum and feedback from your current audience.

Is it possible to start from scratch with a new focus? Absolutely. It just takes longer to build your audience and gain interest from your content, so that is why I encourage you to bridge the gap between your current audience and your future prospects.

Bringing it all Together

Hopefully by now you are starting to get really clear on who your Ideal Avatar is, what your current audience looks like, and are developing the plan to bridge the gap. We will dive into your content and how to engage your Ideal Avatar in the next chapter and it will bring all of this full circle.

But first, let's bring everything together and draw out your Ideal Avatar so we have all of the key components summarized and you can keep her on the forefront for everything that you do. Refer to the graphic at the end of this section and complete each area accordingly.

Goals & Values: List out your Ideal Avatar's goals and what is important to her. Keep in mind how this relates to your product, service or opportunity.

Interests: This is a fun section so you can start to make your Ideal Avatar real. She has books she loves, podcasts she listens to and gurus she follows just like you do. Think of some examples of interests she has and fill them out in this section. My Ideal Avatar likes Target and Whole Foods .

Pain Points: Refer to the section in this chapter where we went over your Ideal Avatar's struggles and pain points. Put the most common ones down here.

Solutions You Offer: When it comes to your product, service or opportunity, how can you solve her struggles and pain points?

Finish this graphic by filling in general demographics about your Ideal Avatar in the middle. Don't worry about being super picky, just some general stats to get clearer on who she is.

Ideal Avatar

Goals & Values

Goals:

Values:

Pain Points

Struggles:

Pain Points:

Interests

Books:

Influences on Social:

Favorite Stores:

Solutions You Offer

Product/Service:

Oppurtunity:

Age:
Gender:
Marital Status:
Kids/Pets:
Annual Income:
Work Experience:

CHAPTER 4

Owning Your Online Space

"Personal branding is the art of becoming knowable,
likable and trustable."

~ John Jantsch

Value vs. Selling

One of the biggest shifts you'll make by working through this book is learning how to lead with value, provide valuable content, and engage your growing audience. The old school way of posting and praying is so '2019'. It just doesn't work anymore.

This couldn't be more true as it is actually against Facebook's™ policies to "sell" on your personal profile. This is why learning how to craft killer curiosity posts is so important as you will learn. But it also drives home the point that you need to learn how to offer value and gain leads that way versus posting about your monthly specials or discounts off of your product kits.

I recruited over 100 people directly to me last year and didn't reach out to a soul. They came to me. When I started analyzing the common thread among all of them, it was that

I had helped them in some way. And I had helped them without expecting anything in return. This is key.

If you have an underlying agenda, they will sense it and it will turn them off. Even without a ton of content like I have out there, you can start mentoring your prospects right away and start offering value from the get go.

One time a girl messaged me and asked if I could watch her online party to give her feedback. I remember it was really late at night and honestly, it was the last thing I wanted to do. But I reminded myself that my goal is to be a servant leader and offer value wherever I can.

I watched the video, gave her honest feedback, and she thanked me and moved on. Later on, she reached out and asked if she could learn more about the company I was with and what it would be like to be on my team.

You may be reading this thinking, *"But Kimberly, I don't have people reaching out to me asking me for guidance."* Well guess what? You can do it anyway! If someone mentions they are trying to follow a keto diet but just love carbs, could you send them some of your favorite recipes you love that take homemade carb-heavy dinners and transform them into magical keto-friendly goodness? Yes!

Could you circle back with someone you've chatted with previously that said she was having a hard time finding time to work out because she homeschooled a bunch of kids and send her a great YouTube video from a mom in a similar situation that had some practical tools she could implement to get results? Yes!

As you can see, the ideas and possibilities are endless, you just have to start looking for ways to love on people without any strings attached. Make it your goal to always come onto social media with the intention of adding value and making people's lives better.

Now, sometimes there will be opportunities to introduce your product, service or opportunity in these examples. You need to pay attention to the feel of your interaction with your potential prospect and see if it makes sense to bring it up.

Let's say someone comments in a Facebook™ Group post and says that they get a second wind at night and stay up way too late and are tired the next day. You could message them with an article you found with five tips to getting to bed at a decent hour and how to transition that last hour so you can fall asleep peacefully.

If the person just says, "Thanks" or gives you a thumbs up, that is not a warm and well-received response. But if they are friendly and appreciative, you could take it to the next step. In our example, you could say, "*Sure thing, those tips really helped me a ton. I also started adding in a clean energy powder that goes right into my water and wow, I haven't needed a nap since I started it. Let me know if you want more info on what it is. Take care!*"

By ending it this way, you are not doing the traditional, "*So, would you be open to taking a look at what I have? If not, no big deal.*" That has been said a million times, right? It's not necessarily bad, but I'd recommend finding the balance between adding value and working into the conversation about what you have to offer.

The bottom line is, with value-driven marketing, you will attract so many leads to you and you won't have to go around pitching yourself to anyone with a pulse.

You will start to learn how to fill up your sales funnel organically with just the content you put out there.

This is what I do and what feels good to me. If you do cold messages all day and love it, then knock yourself out. I pay attention to not only how I feel when I'm sharing what I have, but how I imagine it makes the other person feel. I also think about duplication and what is most attractive to my potential team members.

Keep in mind, most people aren't ready to move forward the first time you "expose" them. So wouldn't you want to make sure they have a good interaction with you?

I do.

Developing Your Personal Brand
Once you get clear on your message, your target audience, and how you want to package what you have to offer, you'll be well on your way to branding yourself successfully.

It's important to learn how to brand yourself and not your company. When you brand yourself, you can take whatever you've built up with you wherever you go. If you are so closely identified with a certain company or product, you lose a ton of traction if you decide to go in a different direction. So whatever you come up with for your brand, keep that in mind.

Before we jump into social media, we need to really hone in on what you want to share with the world. This can be hard for entrepreneurs because we are *so* creative and have *so* many ideas that the concept of narrowing it down to one can be overwhelming.

Let's start with brainstorming what you're good at or what you notice others come to you for advice for (*examples: teaching positive mindset, training on social media, getting out of debt*):

In addition, it is also helpful to consider in broader terms around your company's product line to see how you can cohesively tie that together with your brand and what you want to share (*examples: weight loss/healthy eating/fitness if in health & wellness, body care products if in skincare or makeup, lifestyle for any beauty brands, anti-aging for anything ha ha*):

_____

_____

———————————————————————

———————————————————————

———————————————————————

———————————————————————

———————————————————————

———————————————————————

———————————————————————

———————————————————————

———————————————————————

———————————————————————

Summarize what you want to be known for:

———————————————————————

———————————————————————

———————————————————————

———————————————————————

———————————————————————

Choosing Your Brand Name

Having a brand name is not required for you to build on social media, however, if you want to start to create a personal brand, coming up with a brand name to announce at the beginning and end of Facebook™ Lives, or to put on a quote graphic, can help with your online identity.

You can also just brand yourself, using just your name. Very simple and effective.

I have experience with two strong brands I've picked, *FitKim* and *The Goal Digger Girl*, and both of them came as an inspired idea and I knew instantly they were the ones! But in preparation for that to happen, I kept a notebook with me and browsed around on the internet or in bookstores as often as I could to capture ideas as they came to me. I decided that any name I thought of was worth writing down as it may lead to something even better.

No matter what you decide, make sure it is somewhat obvious what you are all about. It doesn't have to be super descriptive because we'll craft a slogan to go with it that will reveal more details but you want followers to at least get an idea of your theme.

Also, unless you're partnering up with someone, you'll want the brand to be about you and not a "company." People buy from those they know, like, and trust, so centering this concept around your brand is the way to go in my opinion.

You can also use this intel that you're collecting for ideas and inspiration for your personal Facebook™ Group as well.

Take a few minutes to brainstorm some brand names now to get your creative juices flowing and make sure to jot down any more that come to you as soon as they pop into your mind:

_____

_____

_____

_____

_____

_____

_____

_____

_____

Logo Design

And of course, the next best thing to your brand name is your logo! The look and feel of your logo will give followers an instant impression of what you're all about so make sure it is done how you envision it. Communicating what you want can be difficult because you have it in your head but do not settle with your designer.

Write down a few descriptive words of what you want your logo to include (*ie: fun, girly, warm, sassy, playful*):

_____

_____

_____

_____

_____

_____

_____

If possible, put together sample images of other logos you like to give to your designer. You can literally pick and choose, "*I want the font color of this one, the font type of this one, I like the way this one sparkles...*" and on and on. I cannot emphasize enough – do not settle.

Your Slogan

This is your opportunity to tell a short story in just a sentence or two of what your mission is and what you have to offer. This short description of your brand will be used in the about section of your social media profiles, inside of Facebook™ groups, at the bottom of emails and on sales pages. Browse other people's profiles to get ideas but obviously don't copy and paste.

Write down a few here to get you started:

_____

_____

_____

_____

_____

_____

_____

_____

Your Personal Branding Buckets

When it comes to personal branding, the real secret is to learn how to infuse your brand in everything you do, not just post a logo on social media and call it good.

Think about Nike. Yes, we all know the infamous swoosh logo and phrase, "*Just Do It*," but you most likely conjure up associated images and feelings when you think about the brand. For me, I think about living a fit and active lifestyle, setting goals and making them happen. Nike doesn't flat out say that, but it is the underlying messaging.

You will want to do the same thing with the content you create and the conversations you have.

First, you'll want to create five buckets for Facebook™ and/or three buckets for Instagram™. These "buckets" will be areas of your life that you will share through social media such as personal (*selfies, family, etc.*), inspirational, lifestyle, beauty, wellness, parenting, DIY, hobbies, travel or being a girl boss. Think of what can create curiosity so that your followers will want to know about what you do but are also able to get to know you better as a person too!

Facebook™   *Instagram*™

_____   _____

_____   _____

_____   _____

_____   _____

_____   _____

Structure Your Social with Themes

It's not required, but having some sort of theme (*ie:* *#MotivationalMonday*) for each day can be helpful when it comes to deciding what to post on your profiles and in your Stories. Jot down some ideas here:

_____

_____

_____

_____

_____

_____

_____

_____

_____

Plan Your Posts

I recommend posting 1-2 times a day on Facebook™, once a day on Instagram™ and as much as you can in your Stories. Overtime, you can repurpose what you're posting and change it up so that you never run out of content (*or ideas!*). Mix in a variety of post types such as quotes, selfies, polls, curiosity posts and Facebook™ Lives.

We will cover how to plan out your social media in depth, tools you can use, how to create graphics, and more in a later chapter. But this is intended to get you acclimated to what it looks like to plan your social media with more intention around who you are and how you want to show up on social media.

Also, take a look at your plan for the week and make sure you've rotated through all of your buckets so you can continue to share a variety with your followers. Adjust as you go along and you will be well on your way to crushing it on social media and attracting a ton of high quality and HOT leads!

Social Media Content Calendar

Types of posts: Personal, Inspirational, Funny/Entertaining, Opinion, Polls, Educational, Product Posts, Business Posts, Facebook™ Lives

Monday

❏ Done   A.M.   Posts:

_____

❑ Done   P.M.   Posts:

_____

Tuesday

❑ Done   A.M.   Posts:

_____

❑ Done   P.M.   Posts:

_____

Wednesday

❑ Done   A.M.   Posts:

_____

❑ Done   P.M.   Posts:

_____

Thursday

❑ Done   A.M.   Posts:

_____

❑ Done   P.M.   Posts:

_____

Friday

❑ Done   A.M.   Posts:

_____

❏ Done   P.M.   Posts:

_____

Saturday

❏ Done   A.M.   Posts:

_____

❏ Done   P.M.   Posts:

_____

Sunday

❏ Done   A.M.   Posts:

_____

❏ Done   P.M.   Posts:

_____

Mastering Audience Engagement

The name of the branding game is *engagement*. Your entire goal is to create content that your audience interacts with, shares, revisits, and takes action from. You want your followers' lives to be better because of you. The best way to do this is to create content that engages.

The first place to do this is within your posts. I learned this from Erin King, who has become a friend and is author of the amazing book, *Digital Persuasion*. When you're writing your post, look for ways to replace *'I'* with *'you'*. It's tricky at first but once you get the hang of it, you'll start doing it naturally like I do. Here are some examples:

"I am so thankful that I met the man of my dreams and I feel so blessed every day and I truly can't believe how lucky I am."

"Looking forward to celebrating Valentine's Day! How did you meet your special person?"

"I just found out I earned an all expense paid trip to Cabo and I can't wait to go celebrate with my girls!"
"If you earned an all expense paid trip for all of your hard work, where would you go and why?"

Whenever someone is reading your posts, you want them to imagine themselves in your shoes. The only way that can happen is if you use you, your, etc.

I remember when I was contemplating joining my friend's network marketing company for the first time, I honestly didn't think I could replace my income from my corporate job. The belief wasn't there.

However, I started seeing posts from a friend of hers and she was talking about what she was doing during the day while running her online business from home. After following her for a while, I started seeing myself in her shoes.

It was wild, but all of a sudden I shifted from possibly supplementing my income to making it a goal to quit my job and do it full time.

That is your goal with your content. That is what impact you can make on people watching your posts.

Calls To Action

Another important element to master when it comes to engagement is utilizing effective CTAs (Call To Action). This is where you blatantly tell your audience what to do with your content.

Examples:

"Drop ME below if you agree!"

"Type 'GROUP' in the comments if you want me to add you!"

"Just say 'probiotics' if you want to know which ones I use."

I also like to focus on engagement in my Stories, whether it be Facebook™, Instagram™ or both. Look for ways to ask your viewers questions or vote on a poll so they interact. If they comment on a Story, it goes right into messenger!

This is brilliant because they initiated the interaction so technically, they are reaching out to you to start a conversation. Amazing, right?

My last suggestion is to create engagement in your Facebook™ Groups as this is a more intimate setting and you can ask more personal questions to your members.
So if you're wanting to ask some tough questions, get opinions, or start a discussion, Facebook™ Groups are a great way to do that.

How to Build Up Your Know, Like & Trust Factor
When you think about the millions of people in network marketing, online marketing and in coaching businesses, why do people choose you instead of the next person?

Because they like you.

They feel like they know you. And they trust you.

This is the power of social media. You can literally take a completely cold audience, have no friends online, and build up a loyal and engaged audience by implementing what I'm teaching you in this program.

How do I know that?

Because that's exactly what I did.

At first, I was sort of "hiding" behind my FitKim brand. As I mentioned, that was my first experience on social media. I had this persona that was healthy, active, and had it all together when it came to living a healthy lifestyle.

I almost kept up those appearances when I had Addison. I was still rocking the homemade cheerios and everything organic perfection that I touted online.

But then...Elise came.

We did not expect her as soon as we had her in our life and boy, did that take a number on my world. A blessing of course, just completely unexpected.

Now I know God had a bigger plan for me and wanted me to be more relatable and real, but at the time, it was total insanity.

So, when I ventured back onto social media in the fall of 2017, with two in diapers and a totally different person myself, I decided I was going to be completely real.
No more perfection. No more pretending to be someone I wasn't.

I became vulnerable. I shared stories about being a mom and working a full-time job all while trying to build a side hustle from my phone.

I shared my mistakes, my wins, and taught my audience everything along the way.

They loved that I had more dry shampoo in my hair than should be legal.

They loved that I started crying sometimes on my Facebook™ Lives because I was sharing a hurtful time in my life or a story of transformation or I was just so inspired about them changing theirs.

My biggest advice is to be more vulnerable, genuine and authentic. Share the struggles and the successes.

A little side note, if you have your account on friends only on Facebook™ or on private on Instagram™, building on social media will be harder. It doesn't mean you can't, but you will want to work to become public as soon as you can.

The biggest obstacle you will have is not what other people think about you.

Your biggest challenge will be what you think about you.

You will wonder what your husband thinks, your family, your co-workers...the barista at your favorite coffee shop...you name it.

You will.

But once you let go, something magical will happen.

You will start to see that it never really mattered anyway. In fact, you will probably get praise and encouragement from those close to you.

And if not, it doesn't matter. If you won't stand up for your dreams, who will?

Nurturing friendships will also allow you to build up your know, like and trust factor better than anything else.

Message everyone on your Facebook™ friends list the day of their birthday. If you say you're going to send someone something or tag them, do it. Get back to people. Follow up. Be reliable.

If you haven't been reliable in the past, I want you to go stand in the mirror right now and say this out loud (probably good to do anyway!): "*I forgive you for letting some things slip through the cracks. I realize now that I need to be a person of my word and I aspire to build an amazing reputation for myself. I want my prospects to want to buy from me or join my team!*"

Continue to work on how you are showing up to your audience and be consistent.

Trust is such a big piece of this and they need to see you as a reliable and trustworthy leader to decide to follow you, become a customer, client or to join your team.

CHAPTER 5
Let's Get Social

"Content is fire. Social media is gasoline."

~ Jay Baer

Attraction Marketing

I don't know about you, but I honestly cringe when I'm scrolling through the newsfeed and see other network marketers spamming their page day after day. I think this is often why prospects are hesitant about joining because they think they have to do that to be successful and it couldn't be further from the truth.

Instead of trying to convince people to join your team, why not build up your online presence to a place where prospects are coming to you? It really is the best feeling when you have a conversation and they say, *"I've been watching you for a while and I want to know more."* Score! That means you're doing your social media the right way.

It can be a bit overwhelming when you open up your Facebook™ app and sit there wondering what the heck you should post! There is something so vulnerable about sharing what's on your mind – especially original content.

However, once you get the hang of this and learn how to share who you really are and not spam all your friends, you're going to fall in love with the entire process. And a fantastic side effect is a dramatic boost to your visibility on Facebook™ and other social media platforms. So let's dive in!

Attraction Marketing is a term that is now thrown around a lot so let's break it down and look at what it really means. When you think of a brick and mortar business, such as a clothing boutique, think about all the elements involved to draw you in. It would have an appealing sign out front, an attractive display case, friendly and positive employees and showcase its best throughout the store.

Your personal Facebook™ profile is the same thing.

Your profile picture needs to be a clear headshot of yourself, just you, and make sure you don't change this too often (*this is your store sign*). It can be a selfie or a professional shot but get a nice closeup that is easy to see when others see you in post threads or in Messenger. Your cover image can change more frequently, even weekly, as this is your "*display case.*" I love seeing great family shots, vacation destinations or inspirational quotes.

Remove the name of your company and any links to your company page. If people can click the link and go scope it out on their own, why would they need to build a relationship or see what you're all about? In addition, you run the risk of them Googling your company and the majority of network marketing companies have negative stuff floating around the internet about them. Also, not blasting your company name all over the place is part of the attraction which we'll get into shortly with creating curiosity through our posts.

Clean up any old photos from college or anything that is not falling into the fun and classy category. Even though it's your personal profile, we want it set to public viewing so you can get the biggest reach possible, so it needs to be somewhat professional. In addition, I recommend being more like Switzerland when it comes to your opinions because unfortunately there is a lot of emotion one way or the other and that could turn off a potential customer or business partner.

Take the opportunity to complete the 'About' section with a brief description of what you're all about. You can also use a few descriptions that sum up the key attributes you'd like to share. I also love to share any social media links as well so followers can easily find you on other platforms.

Right below the bio section, there are a few more details you can fill out about yourself such as where you are from and where you live. Take advantage of the option to add a website (*any url will be accepted*). I would direct followers to your Facebook™ Group by adding it into this section.

Most importantly, be thinking of what is attractive to others. This isn't about being somebody you're not, but about 'showcasing' your best attributes just like the boutique owner would do in her store. When prospects visit your page, you want them to have a good experience and be drawn to or intrigued to learn more about you. That's what attraction marketing is all about.

Crafting Killer Curiosity Posts

Learning how to craft curiosity posts that you can also infuse into your Facebook™ and Instagram™ Stories is a key foundational piece to organic lead generation. It is worth the effort to keep trying and tweaking until you master this skill set.

Stop the Scroll

Creating curiosity starts with your ability to stop your prospect from scrolling through their newsfeed and stop on your post. The best way to do this is to have an image that grabs their attention and makes them want to see what it is all about. Taking a selfie with a meaningful expression (*surprise, a secret smile, joy*) to reflect the post content is a surefire way to accomplish your goal.

Have a Hook

Work in the pain point you are addressing at the beginning of the post so your prospect can relate immediately to the problem. When you do this, you will help them realize they have a problem and lead them to your solution. Since you are just hinting at the solution, they are much more likely to comment or message you to find out what solved your problem. This is where the curiosity comes into play.

CTAs for the Win

Crafting an awesome post is one thing, but we want your followers to engage. We want them to comment, ask questions, and hopefully say they want more information. A winning strategy to make this happen is to include a CTA (*Call to Action*) either at the beginning of your post or at the very end. As discussed in the previous chapter, a CTA tells your audience what to do. *"Comment below!"*, *"Let me know if..."*, or something such as *"Drop 'ME' if you..."* are all good keywords to use. Play around with your CTA until you see it is doing the job of getting interaction on your posts and go from there.

Creating Curiosity

It took me a few months to really get the hang of curiosity posts so be patient with yourself. Be a student and notice which ones are working and why and check out other people's to get inspiration. Here are some great examples to refer to for ideas and remember to never copy and paste other people's posts.

Kathy Caviness
March 3 at 2:43 PM · 🌐

·>> Anyone else fighting that energy crash mid-afternoon? 😴😴😴
Just me? 🙈😂

👍❤️ Debra Menchel, Tina-Dawa Bacon and 56 others   26 Comments

I was going to cut my hair.

But when Rachelle (my expert stylist The Strand Project) showed me just how long it was . . . I wondered how much longer can it grow?

Honestly, I think this is the longest and the healthiest my hair has been in forever.

If you're curious about what I use and what I do for that shine, let me know.

I'm taking part in a multi-vendor event starting next week (I'm looking at all of you last minute shoppers) where I'll be sharing my hair & skin care secrets.

Am I going to see you there?!

What is the gift you are most excited to give this year?

#spreadingholidaycheer

This year was the first year that when I went Christmas shopping I didn't look at the price tags. It is an incredible feeling

I've worked very hard to get to this point. But in the past I've struggled. I've had to get help from toy drives and others to be able to give my kids a Christmas and to even get a Christmas dinner. And let me tell you, that took a lot to set my pride aside to get that help.

Early in the year, I told my husband I wanted to pay for Christmas myself without his money. I put my head down and I did the work.

I worked even when I didn't think I had the strength to do it.

I worked even when I was so tired I was falling asleep at the computer.

I did it even though I wanted to sit on the couch and watch tv

My point here is that no matter what your dreams and hopes are, put your head down and do the work. You can make ANYTHING happen! You really can.

Crushing Your Facebook™ Lives

Once I got over my fear of doing Facebook™ lives, my business completely changed as well as my confidence in myself and what I had to offer. You want to feel incredible? Start getting comfortable with Facebook™ Lives and eventually expand over to Instagram™ Reels or TikTok too!

Facebook™ announced that its #1 priority for 2018 would be Facebook™ Lives and this has continued to be a top trend. Your lives will get you in front of hundreds if not thousands of people instead of maybe a few dozen on a strong post. In addition, doing lives gives you instant credibility (*like being on TV*) and can help you to have prospects reach out to YOU.

What to cover in your Facebook™ lives is hands down the question I get most often from people and the answer is so much simpler than you'd think. You can have a theme for your lives (*positivity, mindset, inspiration, wellness*) but honestly to start, just start! Ask your friends what they go to you for, notice what you're best at teaching, do a poll or just learn something new and turn around and teach it. Remember, there is always someone you know more than and if you can impact one person, you've done your job.

Whatever you choose, be consistent. Don't go live for five days in a row and then become a ghost for months. Evening times when the kids are in bed is a great time and Facebook™ is very active at night. However, if you want to build a daytime audience then try different times of day and find what works for you!

Let's take a look at some titles for ideas. I definitely encourage you to put some thought into them. I always choose my title ahead of time and save it onto my Trello board so I'm not scrambling right before going live. Use emojis and create curiosity so that people want to know more and hop on to see what your live is all about.

Examples:

"What You Have To Do to Get People to Say YES!" This can help you: (1) know how often to follow up with prospects, (2) know what to say with each exposure and (3) learn how to ask for the sale naturally instead of being spammy. Are you ready?!

"How to Stop Prospecting and Start Recruiting!" Watch this if (1) you have someone interested but then hear crickets, (2) you get a conversation going but can't seem to close them or (3) you just want to enjoy the whole process more!

"Want to know how to have "posture" on social media so you can attract a huge tribe and become a confident closer? Then tune in NOW!"

...

"How to Grow Your Team's Sales with Taprooting and the Power of Duplication!"

...

Be sure to use emojis when it's appropriate!

Jot down topic ideas here and keep a running list as ideas come to you:

_____

_____

_____

_____

_____

_____

_____

_____

Other Tips

- o Have notes prepared because this will keep you on point and prevent you from "squirreling" or rambling. Include your intro (*name/ topic*), your experience with the topic, 3-5 tips, then finish with a call to action.

- o Promote your Facebook™ Live beforehand with a curiosity post in your Stories or by even creating an Event. Share the replay info afterwards in your Facebook™ Groups and Stories as well.

- o Find a designated place that is quiet where you can do your Lives. Have a non-distracting background, a phone stand and good lighting.

- o Go Live on your phone or use software such as Streamyard (my personal favorite). I prefer to schedule mine out so that way I can notify my audience ahead of time and they can opt into the reminder feature.

- o Avoid tagging people in the title unless appropriate; instead do it in the comments. Also, don't put links in the title.

- o Drive up engagement by saying *"Let me know where you are tuning in from!"* or *"On a scale of 1 - 10, how much do you struggle with this topic?"* etc. Most people are replay viewers so don't wait for people to get on when you go live.

- o The length of time depends on the content – mine average 15 to 18 minutes but you can get great content out in less than 10.
- o Respond to every single comment because that will drive up the algorithm and get you in front of more people!
- o Share your new Facebook™ Live on the last three lives you did in the comments section. This will notify your previous viewers about your new content!
- o Think long-term with these and remember the goal is to *become an influencer.* You want to gain their trust, share your journey, and let them get to know who you are and what you have to offer.
- o Focus on helping and teaching, not on the number of views.
- o Embrace #ProgressNotPerfection.

InstaSuccess on Instagram™

All of the principles about Attraction Marketing discussed previously also apply to your Instagram™ account. Rotate through your branding buckets throughout the week. I recommend posting once a day on Instagram™ and as often as you can in your Stories.

Also, there are a few nuances that vary from Facebook™ so I will go over those in this section.

Buying Followers

Now that you know what to post, it's time to start actively building up your following. One tempting strategy to quickly do this is to buy followers. With websites such as Fiverr in your face, it can seem like the way to go. However, Instagram™ has a very sophisticated algorithm and you run the risk of getting your account shut down or at the very least to be put into Instagram™ jail. Also, if followers are inactive for a certain period of time, Instagram™ will automatically cause them to unfollow you after a while so it will only serve you in the short term anyway.

Aggressively Following Others in a Safe Manner

The method that has worked for me to build up my following relatively quickly is to manually and consistently, day in and day out, follow other accounts. It takes a bit of time and you have to be really committed to the process, but it really is worth it. You can also make a game out of it to see how many new followers you can attract daily.

You'll want to find other accounts that are in your niche or something that compliments it. For example, if you're in network marketing, other success-minded / motivational / entrepreneurial type accounts would be a great fit. Find a good account and click on their followers. Go through and check the profile image and name and make sure they look like someone you'd want to follow. Do not scroll down and follow as many as you can, as fast as you can. That will flag Instagram™ and get you into trouble. Instead, follow no more than 50-100 an hour and go through them organically, not quickly like a bot. Follow no more than 200 total daily.

Once I got my account to where I was following several hundred people, I started unfollowing people as I was adding new accounts to follow. You don't want to be following way more people than are following you. Also note that the max you can follow is 7,500.

You can reuse your Instagram™ post onto Facebook™ or vice versa. You can also share your Instagram™ URL to your page or group and call it #FridayFollow where you encourage everyone to follow each other's accounts.

Hashtag #Hashtag

It's time to tackle the elusive topic of hashtags. Yes, they are important. They can help potential followers find you that wouldn't have otherwise. If you can rank up in the top of certain hashtag categories, it can help you to become viewed as an influencer. You can also use them specifically to promote contests, giveaways, raffles, campaigns – you name it. Always search it first to see how competitive the space is for that specific hashtag.

The max number of hashtags to use per post is 30, with 11-15 seeming to be the sweet spot for algorithm ratings. I like to bury mine in the comments so my posts look cleaner from the start. Try to change them up and have some relevant ones for that specific post each time too. Use a hashtag app for ideas and look at other people's posts to get inspired. I save all of mine in my notepad app on my phone and just pick and choose based on the theme of my post.

Find your best hashtags by posting and then going over to the search field to see if you show up in the top results for that specific hashtag. If it's a super popular hashtag, it doesn't make sense to use it if you're not going to show up in the results, unless it is specifically part of the wording for your post description. Play around with it and save the best ones. Also, throw in geotags (*tagging a location*) once or twice a week as they get up to 79% more engagement than regular posts!

Becoming an Influencer

I definitely believe that actively growing your follower list should be something that you are very involved in and work at daily, but I also like to work smarter, not harder. Here is where influencers come into play. This is where you either do a promotional exchange (*shout out for shout out*) or you actually pay to have a very big influencer shout you out. You can even start with those in this group or in your engagement pods that have a similar number of followers and niches that compliments one another.

Even if you're just starting out, you can quickly become an influencer by showing up consistently, offering great content and by interacting with your followers. You want to get to a place where your followers look forward to your next post. You want them to turn on their post notifications and always stop scrolling through the newsfeed when they see your name. The best way to do that is to focus on three topics and rotate through them as you post.

Instagram™ Lives + IGTV + Instagram™ Reels
The other place to really stand out is by doing Instagram™ Lives. You'll actually go Live inside of your stories and it'll stay up for 24 hours. You do have the option to save it and I highly recommend doing that so you can repurpose it on Facebook™ or as an IGTV. For anyone that comments, you can reply back and it goes right into their inbox which is awesome. I love the filters they have too.

Next to the Instagram™ scene is *IGTV*. The intention was to model YouTube's format and eventually offer influencers a space to monetize their content. What's nice is you can take the videos from IGTV and easily share them to Facebook™ or vice versa because they are pre-recorded. An amazing feature they have now is the ability to share it to your Instagram™ profile feed and your followers can click more to view your entire video on IGTV. I really like that they stay up and users can easily scroll through all your videos and pick and choose what they'd like to view.

And trailing quickly behind the launch of TikTok came Instagram™ Reels. Although the features on TikTok are better in my opinion, it is easier to have your Reel get a lot of eyes on it versus the crowded space on TikTok.

I personally create on TikTok, remove the watermark after it is posted, then upload to Reels. I average over 125,000 views monthly from my Reels and they are only 15 seconds in length! It is a fantastic way to generate new leads in such a short period of time.

Instagram™ Highlights

By using branded colors and catchy titles, you can give your followers even more reason to hang out on your page and

you will also get more leverage out of your old Stories.

Presets & Filters

The "*look*" of your Instagram™ account is just as important as what you actually post. Instagram™ is all about images and having a certain look and feel to your account. This will help tell your followers a lot about you. Do you want to have a beachy tone, a cool black and white feel, or a comfy rose-gold infused look? The best way to get consistency on your page is by finding a specific preset or filter that you use for all of your photos. I like VSCO and Lightroom the most but I highly recommend having a custom preset made so you can get the exact look you are going for.

Facebook™ and Instagram™ Stories

If I could choose one area of social media for you to really master, it would be Facebook™ and Instagram™ Stories. I was just reading how Instagram™ Stories are being viewed *triple* the amount of the posts shown in the newsfeed. That's powerful. Also, Facebook™ and Instagram™ love it when you use all of their various features and will favor you within the algorithm when you venture into Stories.

When you think of Facebook™ and Instagram™ Stories, I want you to think about being behind the scenes of a movie set. You know how neat it is to see what it really takes to create a movie or what actors and actresses have to do to make it all happen? It's the same thing with your Stories. You want to give your followers a glimpse into your day-to-day activity, ranging from a minimum of four Stories a day up to dozens. Maybe you share a sweaty selfie in the morning, an awesome new smoothie recipe you've tried for the first time, and then show a curiosity post about your product later that day.

Capture images throughout your day and sit down at once to design your Stories and post them once or twice a day. Use apps such as StoryChic or InStories to bring your Stories to life and grab viewers' attention. Utilize the engaging features offered such as creating a poll, asking a question or putting a quiz together to get qualified leads galore!

I like to use Snapchat to record short video clips or take a selfie because the filters are outstanding. Instagram™ will automatically slice up your Stories into 15 second clips otherwise use the app 'Continual' if you are going straight to Facebook™. Another great app is InShot because you can add backgrounds, music, speed up or slow down a video, etc.

Apps are your friend when it comes to Instagram™ and Facebook™ Stories! I'll be honest, just like Facebook™ Lives, it does take some time to get the hang of what to put in your Stories and to keep it consistent with what you're posting on your personal profile. But, if you're diligent with the process, consistent, and willing to have some fun, you're going to get *so* much more exposure and a ton of new leads. Everyone who views your Story is a potential lead. And they actively clicked your Story to take a look at what's happening in your life, versus reactively seeing what you've posted that comes up in their newsfeed. That's major leverage.

CHAPTER 6

Make it Sizzle

"People do not buy goods and services. They buy relationships, stories, and magic."

~ Seth Godin

Prospect Management

When I first joined my network marketing company, I reached out to a ton of people via text or on Facebook™ Messenger. Most responded with some sort of interest so it was my responsibility to follow up with them. There were so many messages here and there that a lot of people fell through the cracks. I quickly realized I needed some sort of system to keep track of everyone and follow up accordingly.

There are three main formats I've seen that work in this industry but of course find what works for you. Here's a brief summary of each to get you started.

Paper: with this method, all leads go onto a master list in a notebook. Once they become a prospect (after you've exposed them to your product or company), they are then moved to another section in the notebook for follow up, one area for potential customers and one for potential business builders. Customers can be moved to another section as well as business partners that join your team.

The upside to this method is that when we write something down, we make a connection to it in more of a creative way than just typing it. Also, it's nice because you can *"see"* all of your leads right in front of you at all times. However, it is extremely cumbersome to move your names throughout the different sections, keep track of when to follow up with them and you also lose the ability to sort the list by common denominators such as last follow up date.

Digital Spreadsheets: using programs such as Asana, Google Sheets or Trello (*because #TrelloIsLife*) helps to capture all of your leads digitally but *you* are in charge of manually tracking them. You can create different columns or even tabs to identify your leads, prospects, customers and business partners. The way you want to set up the format is completely up to you. Also, an app is available for most systems.

[Check the book resources at **thegoaldiggergirl.com/bossitup** to get a copy of my Google

Sheets and Trello Prospecting Tracker if you haven't already.]

With Trello, you can automate the follow-up process by setting reminders that will allow you to actually remember to reach back out. Another neat feature is that you can link your contact's name directly to their Facebook™ profile for easy accessibility. Outside of that, you are responsible for keeping up with your list on a daily basis.

Online Programs: there are many online programs available for contact management but I'll just touch on one because I've used it a ton and love it. GroupTrack is an online system that syncs right up to Facebook™ and is designed to help you stay organized with your contacts. Another one that some of our students like is Teamzy and it was built by network marketers so may be worth looking into.

Whichever system you choose, take your initial list that you created with your warm leads and put everyone on there that you can possibly think of. Go through your cell phone contacts and Facebook™ friends and add them to your prospect list. You'll want this list to be in the hundreds. Think big! I'll teach you how to add tons of new leads to this list and soon we'll go through the process to turn them into a warm prospect.

Passionate Prospecting

The questions I get most often from my audience are about how to recruit people online. There is a lot of bad information out there, confusion and straight up anxiety around the whole topic. So hang in there and not only will I show you how to do it the right way (*in my humble opinion*), I will also show you how to enjoy the entire process and actually look forward to your next interaction. And remember, your opportunity is a potential blessing to others and we're *not* in the business of convincing people.

Posture

When you're connecting with potential customers and business builders, it's extremely important that you practice coming from a place of abundance instead of lack. People will absolutely respond differently to you based on your mindset. Take control of the conversation, have confidence in yourself and be an authority in the situation. You want to be seen as a leader. Even if you have to fake it until you make it, that is how you will need to go about it for now.

I recommend incorporating daily mindset practices where you visualize people saying yes, your team growing quickly, and for you to open up your inbox and it's full of prospects saying they want to know more! It may seem silly, but it absolutely works. And really what do you have to lose?

Starting the Conversation

I'm going to assume you've already worked through your warm market and if you haven't already, exhaust that list first before moving onto cold leads. Cold leads cannot be prospected until they've become warm, so you'll almost always be at an advantage working through true warm leads before moving onto cold leads. And for those of you reading this that are thinking, *"I've burned out my warm market,"* you can build a new warm market right on social media.

When it comes to cold leads, the best ones to prospect are the ones that proactively interact with you and open up the door to a conversation. This will come in various ways such as someone sending you a friend request, watching your Facebook™ Story or commenting/liking/reacting to your posts. Even better are those that share your posts!

If they send you a friend request, or accept yours, message them back and say something such as, *"Thanks for the friend request – I love connecting with new people on Facebook™. I saw your adorable girls – I have two as well. I'd love to get to know you better – tell me a bit about yourself!"* Continue getting to know them until you can find a pain point and bring up your business opportunity or product. We'll cover exactly what to say in a bit.

If they interacted with one of your posts, Lives or Stories, you can message them and say, *"Hey, there! I saw (insert whatever action they took), what was your favorite part?"* Remember, you're the expert, so look for opportunities to mentor them since they are proactively digesting your content.

One of my favorite places to connect with like-minded people are in Facebook™ groups, as discussed previously. If someone interacts with your comment or post, they are a lead. If they comment on a post in the group and you really like what they've contributed, you can reach out to them via messenger, *"Hey, there! I'm also in the Women Helping Women group and I loved what you said about trading time for money – how long have you been an entrepreneur?"*

The reason why I love sending birthday messages (*text, voice memo or send a video*), is because not many do it but also because it's a great way to connect with every single person on your friends list. If they don't respond back, I delete them. If they do, I connect with them, build rapport and look for a way to share what I have to offer. *"I just realized we've been friends for a while and haven't connected yet. Tell me a bit about yourself!"*

One of the most powerful ways to find new people to prospect is through referrals. We know it but we forget to make it a regular part of our business. Ask one of your current customers to host an online party and invite all their friends. My favorite way is to share my company's referral program with current customers and ask who they know that could also benefit from the product or business. Ask them to do a referral curiosity post for you about your product and handle anyone who comments on their post for them.

What to Say

Here are some Do's and Don'ts when it comes to prospecting:

- o Don't ever copy and paste a script. Facebook™ knows you're doing it, your prospects know you're doing it and you know you're doing it. It's a lose-lose all around. I'd rather you read a script on voice messenger if you're that unsure of what to say.

- o Never become defensive or rude if they're not interested or respond negatively.
- o Find their pain point and tweak your story accordingly.
- o Use voice messenger whenever possible.
- o Use 3rd party validation tools such as videos, testimonials, PDFs or private Facebook™ groups.
- o When you're new, work towards a three way chat so your upline can assist you.
- o Don't prospect everyone – be selective about who you're recruiting and think long-term.

Crafting Your Sizzling Story

This can take some time to get the hang of, but you'll want to craft your unique story. Ideally, it's less than 60 seconds in length so you can keep people's attention easily. Also, try to tweak it based on the prospect's background/situation/pain points. Here's an example of mine:

1. *Who you are and where you've been*: I'm a busy mom with two young kiddos; I have been working

full-time and running a couple of businesses nights and weekends to make ends meet.

2. *What's happened in your life to cause you to look for something more (WHY were you open)*: Because I was working so much, I missed Elise's first steps and began looking for a way to be home more and still make a great income.

3. *How you heard about your company and why you had to be a part of it*: My friend introduced me to her products and shared how much they were helping people. She'd completely replaced her income from her full time job and was driving a shiny, white Cadillac. I quickly realized this would be the way for me to make my transition to working from home.

4. *Why you're excited/What's next*: Since then I've grown a team of thousands, become completely debt free and now have a very flexible schedule that I love. And I get to teach others to do the same!

The Four Color Personalities

Have you ever recruited someone and just couldn't figure them out, or worse, not be able to motivate them? Or have you been having a conversation with a prospect and they seemed interested but then they became silent or said no all of a sudden? This is most likely because they are a completely different color than you so it's your job to learn these well for yourself and for those that you lead!

Yellow: "The Helper"

o Loves giving hugs to strangers

o Everyone loves them and trusts them

o Not interested in the compensation plan

o Wants to know if the products help people

o Great servant leaders

o Doesn't like being bossed around

o Great at relationships

Blue: "Let's Party"

o Loves fun, travel, and adventure

o Loves meeting new people

o Talks to everyone, always talking

o Natural promoters, i.e.: *"gotta see this movie!"*

o Network marketing is a perfect fit

o They don't listen well; mind is going in a million directions

o Not great at following up, too busy meeting new people

Red: "Bossy"

- o Wants to be in charge
- o Organized, tells others what to do
- o Wants results, can't stand people whining with excuses
- o Will make the most money
- o Their way or the highway attitude
- o Wants you to get the job done and doesn't want your input
- o Gets things done
- o Very competitive, loves trophies and recognition

Green: "Information"

- o Loves data
- o Not much emotion
- o Logical, typically wants more info
- o Loves spreadsheets, analytics, collecting data and pondering
- o Likes to think of all the future scenarios
- o Spends too much time thinking vs. taking action
- o Wants to be able to answer any question from prospects/team

You'll naturally be drawn to people with similar personalities but will experience tremendous growth when you master leading and developing different personalities. You can find more info from the book, *The Four Color Personalities for MLM.*

The Fortune is in the Follow Up

One of the biggest mistakes newbie network marketers make is not following up. When someone says no, not interested or goes silent, they take it personally and become fearful about reaching back out. What they don't know is that most people are just busy and forget to respond back or are just not ready right now. Psychologically, people need to be *"exposed"* many, many times before saying yes to anything.

As Eric Worre says in the book *Go Pro*, "The fortune is in the follow up." You'll want to come up with a creative way to follow up. Examples are: follow up on a video you sent them, a sample, a PDF document, a flash sale, an event, a new product, or offering the business opportunity if you lead with the product or vice versa, etc. Whatever you choose to follow up with, schedule your next follow up immediately or you will forget!

Which one do you want to be?

- 48% of people NEVER follow up with a new prospect
- 25% of people make a second contact and then stop
- 12% of people only make three contacts and stop
- ONLY 10% make more than three contacts
- 2% of sales are made on the first contact
- 3% of sales are made on the second contact
- 5% of sales are made on the third contact
- 10% of sales are made on the fourth contact
- 80% of sales are made on the fifth to twelfth contact

CHAPTER 7

The Attractor Factor

"Build a lifestyle around your brand, and the audience will follow."

~ Eva Chen

Content Creation

Instead of reaching out to your same old leads list yet again, start working on creating awesome content that naturally generates leads. Wouldn't it be more fun to grow your business organically by attracting prospects to you instead of having to reach out to people over and over again?

This isn't to be lazy, it's to be savvy. It's to learn how to leverage the greatest tool we have at our fingertips as online marketers – social media. We have already discussed curiosity posts, Facebook™ Lives, and Stories, but let's break that down a bit more so you can see exactly how to turn your content into a lead-generating-machine.

Profile Posts

With the posts you put on Facebook™, you can rotate between indirect and direct posts to attract leads to you. An indirect post would be a post such as:

- Would you rather have more time or more money?

- Would you rather lose weight or have more energy?
- Fill in the blank: When it comes to my (hair/skin/nails), I wish _____.
- Finish this sentence, If I had a million dollars, I would _____.

Our goal isn't to work in our product or business, but to be able to have a reason to create a conversation in messenger and see if you can turn that lead into a prospect.

For example, if you used the indirect post, *"When it comes to my hair, I wish…"* and someone responded *"I wish it was thicker!"* then you could easily reach out and share how your products help you or your customers grow their hair back.

Or for the million dollar question, when someone answers *I would pay off all my student loans,* you could reach out and share how you are/or have paid off your debt with your online business, and could you get them some more info on how you're doing it via social media?

Facebook™ Lives

My favorite way to build relationships and establish myself as an authority figure is by looking for ways to mentor my viewers. To start, message each viewer that commented or reacted to your video and say, *"Hey NAME! Thanks for watching my live on XYZ, what did you like most?"* When they answer, look for an opportunity to offer an additional piece of value such as tagging on another video that compliments the topic, sending an article you read or a great YouTube video.

Now, how do you circle back to what you do? If they mention a pain point right off the bat, just follow the guidelines of what you have already learned in this program to share how your product/service/opportunity helps solve that problem and go into your sales funnel.

However, if it doesn't naturally come up, work it into what you are talking about. Let's say you do a live on how to lose weight through mini meals, and you reach out to a lead and they say they loved it because they are always looking for ways to keep things creative in the kitchen. You could say, *"I am the same way! I actually became a health and wellness influencer a couple of years ago because I just love simple ways to help others feel their best. Have you tried XYZ before?"* Or you could say, *"I am the same way! How long have you been working on a healthy lifestyle?"* And when they tell you, you could say you love sharing clean products that help others stick to their health goals, and get permission to send more information.

Facebook™ & Instagram™ Stories

The easiest ways to get leads from your Stories is by utilizing the poll feature or directing viewers to send you a DM. When you are new, you can capture every single Story viewer as a lead and put them on your tracker. Reach out and connect with them about the particular Story they viewed and follow the steps mentioned in the previous section. If they view a Story that makes zero sense to connect on, you can message them and say, *"Hey, NAME! Thanks for checking out my Stories. I would love to connect and get to know you better. Can you tell me a bit about yourself? Looks like we have a lot in common!"*

With the poll feature, the biggest piece of advice I can give you is to be organized and capture every single response on your prospecting tracker. You can access poll results after 24 hours by going to the archived section on both Facebook™ and Instagram™. Just remember to make both answers positive such as *Yes* and *Of Course* or refer to either or choices outlined at the beginning of this section.

If you are consistent with your content, you should be generating dozens and dozens of new leads every week. By implementing a solid follow-up system, you will be a very busy online marketer.

Friends & Followers

If you have more than a few hundred friends or followers, then you really should never feel like you have no one to talk to. There are always ways you can reach out and strike up a conversation.

On Facebook™, download your Friends List which can be found by going to *Settings > Your Facebook™ Information > Download Your Information*. Pull up your Friends List and go through each contact to see if you have shared with them before. For older contacts, invite them into your Facebook™ Group.

For warmer contacts that you haven't talked to in a while, invite them to an online event. For newer connections, message them and say, *"Hey NAME! I just realized we have been friends on Facebook™ for some time here and we haven't connected. I'd love to get to know you better – can you tell me a bit about yourself? It looks like we have a lot in common!*"

On Instagram™, when you go to your Followers list, you can sort it (*at the time of me writing this*) by clicking where it says '*Sort by Default*' and you'll see an up and down area, click that and choose Earliest. It'll show you who you have been following the longest first and vice versa if you choose Latest. There is also software out there that will let you export your *entire* Instagram™ following. Amazing, right?

A *key* component to making this whole list building thing work is by making new connections every single day. You need new eyes on your content consistently otherwise you're going to be beating a dead horse by trying to reach out with the same people over and over again.

But, not anymore! By following these simple strategies, I grew my Facebook™ Friends List from 250 to 5,000 and my Instagram™ from nothing to over 40,000. You can do this too. And the beautiful thing is it only takes one new follower or friend to turn into a new customer or business builder for you to be on the path to success!

Gaining Awesome Leads through Customer Referrals

What if I told you it was possible to build your business exponentially without reaching out to a cold lead ever again? I know, I know – it sounds really pie in the sky...but I have good news because it is totally possible.

Think back to your first Mary Kay event or similar home party and remember how the consultant would have you meet with her one-on-one to go over your product wish list and have you book a party of your own? She would walk out of there with several new parties on her calendar and that was from just *one* event!

With the power of social media, you can literally 10x these results. To start, make sure you check in on your new customer and help them get started correctly. If they are happy, they are way more likely to refer you to others obviously.

Once they confirm they are experiencing positive results, ask them if they will do a referral post for you. Say, *"I am so glad you are loving the products and would love to help you get some for free! The best way to do this is with a simple post on social media. I will help you write it and handle anyone who comments with interest, and of course you will get credit for them. Can we make that happen?"*

Help them write the post and choose an appropriate picture of themselves. For each person that comments, have them put you in a chat with the prospect and say, *"Hey NAME! This is my friend Kimberly, she can tell you more about these awesome products that have helped me with XYZ."* Handle everything and make it super easy for the person to refer people to you. If you don't have a reward system for customers, make up your own.

Aleshia Wisch
March 20 at 7:21 PM · 🌐

You guysssss!!!!! My friend, Kathy Caviness showed me these MAGNETIC LINER AND LASHES & I had to have them!!! 😍 😍

And you all know how bad I am at things like this...and if I can do them, I KNOW you can too! 💜

Look how pretty... and they're simple too!! 😉

If you want in, let me know 🙌 & she will send you info!

Stephanie Lafler
April 5 at 8:17 AM · 🌐

Had a friend at the gym ask me once... are those dip? Nope, just actual nail polish strips a good friend hooked me up with 💅. So simple I did these while on a zoom call last night 😄

157

After that, the next step is to ask them to hold an online event for you (aka the 15 Minute Facebook™ Party). *"Hey, NAME! If you could earn a free product, would you be willing to host an online party? Mine are short and sweet (15 minutes) and then I'd keep the party open for 48 hours!"* Refer to the scripts in my 15 Minute Facebook™ Party 2020 Workshop for additional support.

An advanced strategy is to share your customers' success stories for them (*with their permission of course*) and handle the leads directly. You can post on your profile or in your Stories. Utilize screenshots of their texts or messages (*including voice*) so you have a genuine testimonial for social proof.

Making the Most of Your Online Events

Getting a party on the books or a sneak peek is a great first step, and we want to make sure you make the most of it so you can leverage your time properly and get the results you are looking for. Once you book with your hostess, the key is to prepare her properly on how the party will work and her role in it. Her excitement and engagement will be a huge factor in the overall success of the party so this step is critical.

Give her scripts to use to invite her friends and then walk her through what to do next. Once everyone is invited and in the group, create an Event inside the group and invite all guests. Ideally, have her remind her guests privately before the party starts or tag anyone that doesn't get on live right away or immediately after. If you can give her some sort of incentive for the size of the party sales, she is way more likely to work her guest list to help you rock it!

Teach your hostess how to create 3 way chats whenever someone engages in the party in any way. Even a simple introduction will allow you to thank them for participating in the party and be able to ask them about their struggles (*ie: pain points*) and open up the conversation.

Create a real party incentive that ends 48 hours after the party begins with the Facebook™ Live kickoff. Stress urgency by following up privately with each party guest.

Once the raffle winner is chosen and announced, offer free shipping to them if there are any other products they would like to get and often they will want to place an order too!

After the party is complete, ask each party member that engaged within the group if they would like to host their own online event to receive product credit. This is an awesome strategy whenever someone has an initial money objection as well. If you can get several online events on your calendar monthly and work those leads, you will have hundreds of new warm prospects filling up your tracker! We also teach you how to automate these online parties inside the 15 Minute Facebook™ Party Workshop.

Kimberly Olson added a 3D photo.
March 26 at 4:27 PM

Yep it's true. Unicorns 🦄 do love coffee and I love having a business that is truly magical. March will be my second biggest income month...ever. How? Simple systems that duplicate 🙌 🙌.

Last chance to check out my sneak peek event to see why my company is different. Sprinkle some 💜 love below if you want an invite 😊.

Now, for the business side, you will want to occasionally book a sneak peek event so you and your team can invite prospects to take a look at your opportunity. This can be via Zoom, inside a Facebook™ Group, or event by utilizing a number to call in and listen.

Choose the date and time and give your team a script to use to invite people. Have everyone create a curiosity post as well. You can do a giveaway, such as an Amazon gift card, if you want to sweeten the pot.

During the sneak peek, share a bit about the company, why you got involved, what makes it special, and how those interested can get started. Create some urgency with a bonus training if they sign up by a certain date if you want (*ie: 48 hours*). Remember to tell them to get back with the person who invited them to learn more.

Blowing Up Your Leads List with Challenges

If I could think of one way to get the most leads at once it would be through a really great challenge. The nice thing about challenges is that you can offer a ton of value but easily work in your products/service/opportunity by tying it right into the content.

To effectively run a challenge, follow these steps:

1. Choose a date range and topic that goes hand-in-hand with your niche. For example, if you are in health and wellness, you could run a water, step, or healthy eating challenge. It's a little trickier with something like beauty so, you could go the self care route or pamper yourself – just get creative.

2. Create the Event inside of your team's Facebook™ Group that you use for prospects or create a stand alone pop up group for the challenge. Give your team scripts (*Evernote is easy to share*) and sample curiosity posts so they know how to individually invite for the challenge.

3. For the event description, be as clear as possible and also go live inside the group explaining the challenge if possible. Have your leaders contribute to a giveaway with extra product they have if you can.

Kimberly Olson
March 20 at 2:35 PM · 🌐 ▾

I don't know about you but I could really use a distraction right now 😌. So I'm jumping into a five day healthify your home challenge starting Monday. $500+ in prizes - wanna do it with me 🙌 ??

[With extra time at home right now, what better way to make the most of it other than with a healthify your home challenge?!

For five days, we will give you ideas and action steps to tackle a variety of areas right at home so you can knock out that spring cleaning and feel totally refreshed!

Daily prizes will be awarded just for completing your homework *with   a   value   of   over $500!*

To register, RSVP to this event, comment below I'M IN and tag the person who invited you! Do a post on your wall for an extra entry   into   the   drawings!

Every day we will post a homework feed so you can check in and have a chance to win prizes!]

4. Ask your teammates to take turns going live or you can do it if you are starting out. Do a value-based training sharing tips that go with the challenge and mention products when possible. You don't have to be pitchy and mention the product name, just say if you want to know which product we recommend (*ie: insert type of product such as dry shampoo, serum, probiotic*), say '*more info*' in the comments and tag the person who invited you.

5. Create a homework post each day and let your challengers check in. If you want to keep it really simple I have also just told them to check in throughout the challenge in the events tab discussion area and say "*All done!*" at the end to register for the prizes. Either way works!

6. Whatever you choose for the challenge, make it easy and open ended. For example, don't say you must do 100 burpees for five days in a row to complete the challenge. Instead do something such as: choose a daily goal for physical activity or a daily water intake amount to shoot for and mark it complete each day. You can also do custom daily action steps that go along with the Facebook™ Live trainings such as: wash your makeup brushes and let them air dry properly to complete today's challenge.

7. Challenge length can vary but it doesn't have to be long – I have seen three day challenges totally rock! If done properly, your Facebook™ group can double in size and your team's sales numbers can skyrocket. How awesome is that?!

CHAPTER 8

Your Boss Babe Community

"You don't earn loyalty in a day. You earn loyalty day-by-day."

~ Jeffrey Gitomer

Purpose of a Facebook™ Group

You most likely either *know* you need a Facebook™ Group or have one that is limping along. If it is already rocking, you can use this chapter to take your results to the next level. Either way, understanding the purpose of having the Facebook™ Group is extremely important so you have purpose and direction when it comes to running one.

The underlying purpose of any Facebook™ Group, no matter the niche or industry, is to make your group member's life easier or more fulfilled. This can come in the form of inspiring, educational, completely community-based or anything else you can think of to make life better.

I do recommend that your first group be non-selling versus creating a group sharing all about your products/services/opportunity. This is because we will want a place to build up your know, like, and trust factor with your prospects and we can do this much easier in a value-based Facebook™ Group versus a traditional customer VIP group.

Starting and running a Facebook™ Group takes work so I would only get one up and running at a time. Once you get the value-based group up then you can work alone or with your team to create a customer driven group later on.

Going back to Chapter 3, think about your ideal avatar and what type of group you could create to make her life better or more fulfilled. You also want to keep in mind you will be creating content consistently for this group so it should also be aligned with something you are very interested in or passionate about. Complete the following section to get clarity on your Facebook™ Group and remember we can pivot down the road if we need to (*this is just a jumping off point*):

My   Facebook™   Group   Name:

_____

_____

My   Community   will   be   based   around:

_____

_____

People will want to join my Facebook™ group because:

_____

_____

What solution am I offering to my members:

_____

_____

When choosing your name, remember your tagline you came up with previously and see how you can work that in or be inspired by it.

Filling Up Your Facebook™ Group

Aside from determining what your group name will be and what it will be about, know that learning how to fill your group up and continuing to grow it will be essential to your long-term success. I had 100 people in my very first group in the fall of 2017 and at the time of writing this, I now have well over 40,000 members in my groups and have built up to almost three million dollars in revenue by utilizing Facebook™ Groups. So let's jump in!

Here are 18 ways to fill them up! We will flesh this out as we go but I wanted you to have them all in one place. You obviously don't have to do them all but go ahead and circle your top three you will start with.

1. Facebook™ Post
2. Facebook™ Stories
3. Instagram™ Post
4. Instagram™ Stories
5. Facebook™ Live
6. IGTV
7. LinkedIn Connections
8. TikTok Leads
9. YouTube Videos with CTA
10. Work through Others
11. Facebook™ Friends List
12. Birthday Messages
13. New Friend Requests
14. New Instagram™ Followers
15. Email List
16. Post Group on Facebook™ Profile
17. Post Group on Instagram™ Profile
18. Run Facebook™ Ads

Before you start inviting, you will want to get clear on the top pain points you will be solving. As you have learned, you need buckets of content to rotate through to give your social media consistency and start to establish your credibility in your space. The same thing goes for your Facebook™ Group. I personally run a social media content plan for each of my groups based on the nature of the group and obviously the solutions I want to offer. Refer to book resources at **thegoaldiggergirl.com/bossitup** to get a copy of my Facebook™ Groups Social Media Content Calendar.

Specifically for your Facebook™ Group, what are the *top 3 pain points* of your prospects?

1. _____

_____

2. _____

_____

3. _____

_____

Once you have dropped in a few posts so the group content isn't completely empty, you can start inviting one-on-one when the opportunity arises. Say something such as, "*Hey NAME, I'd love to get you an invite to my Facebook™*

Group called XYZ which is all about [insert solution solving problem]. I think you'll love it! Can I get you in there?"

In addition, the fastest way to fill up a group or get a huge surge in numbers is by hosting a free challenge (*covered in the last chapter*), an awesome freebie or with a giveaway.

If I could choose one, I would personally start with a challenge because those not only get your prospects in there, but they also get them engaged and used to checking in with the group on a daily basis. Facebook™ defaults to group members' notifications being set to *"highlights"* so they typically will only see your group notifications a few times a week. However, if they are registered for an event in the group, they will get notified every day! Habits are formed and you now have a loyal and engaged group member.

My next suggestion would be to create a great freebie (*ie: lead magnet*) and promote it outside of the group and draw people in that way. We will go into *great* detail around lead magnets later on, but I want you to draw upon content you already have or something that would be easy for you to create. See my list of ideas below to get you started!

And my last suggestion outside of individual reach outs is *a giveaway*. You can give away a book, some girl boss swag or something even more enticing such as a Target or Starbucks gift card. Remember, this is an advertising expense and is part of you investing in your business to grow it so think strategically on it. Giveaways tend to work best when your group is up and running and you can ask current group members to invite their friends to the group to get more drawings for the giveaway. Try out a few different ways and just be patient with the whole process. It takes time to get groups going!

THE Goal Digger Girl's

LEAD MAGNET
Cheat Sheet

One of the best ways to begin developing a loyal following is by offering a value-packed freebie. In the marketing world, this is commonly referred to as your Lead Magnet. Here are some of my favorite ideas to get you started!

eBook: I know this sounds super fancy but it is as simple as putting together some helpful tips in Word, designing a cover in Canva and then saving it as a PDF. Voila! I also like to create a 3D image to promote it to increase the perceived value.

Video Training: When you put together great content in a video training, why not reserve it for a special offer to your new subscribers? You can upload a Facebook or Instagram Live to YouTube or record one from scratch.

Quizzes/Surveys: This lead magnet has a very high conversion rate because people are very curious – especially about themselves! Check out tryinteract.com to get started.

Webinar: These are a bit more advanced, but scheduling leads to attend a "live" webinar through a service such as easywebinar.com will sky-rocket the perceived value and help you gain some highly qualified prospects onto your list.

Cheat Sheet: Just like this one I have given to you, you can organize tips into a checklist, tracker or a list of some sort. These are also received really well because people are so busy, they just love the simplistic format!

There are many other ideas as well, limited only to your creativity, but these are a great starting point and definitely my fav!

Creating Engaging Content

Aside from filling up your group, the next area to conquer is creating content that is engaging. It is completely normal for a small percentage of people to engage on your content so don't let that deter you. Remember, Facebook™ is picking and choosing what content to share with your members in their notifications so it will be hit or miss in regards to what they see.

Just as you learned previously, you will want to create content by asking questions, creating polls, giving choices, inspiring, entertaining, and educating. And don't forget your Facebook™ Lives! I would go live once a week in your group and try to make it a certain day so they can start expecting you. If you can get really fancy and have a set day and time you could even put that in your group cover which would be really amazing for increased participation!

Here are five ways to crush your content:

✔ *Follow a Content Calendar:* see below for a very simple themed content calendar or refer to my FB Groups Content Calendar Trello Board in the resources section.

✔ *Go Live weekly*: I already recommended weekly and remember to promote your Facebook™ Live topic outside of the group on social media and in your Stories. You can use your Lives as an opportunity to plug your products, services, and opportunities indirectly by mentioning them briefly. But they should overwhelmingly be value-driven.

✔ *Include CTAs*: Calls To Action are an-going strategy you will want to implement to encourage engagement with your posts and Lives.

✔ *Promote Replays with the Poll Feature*: You can utilize the poll feature and post the link to the replay of your Live you already did that week or even revive ones from previous weeks as traction usually dies off within a few days. Pick a discussion topic based off the live and watch how it really gets a discussion going!

✔ Add Value with Guest Trainers: Regularly bringing in guest trainers as a reward for the group achieving certain milestones such as the number in the group is an awesome way to add value and credibility to your group. You can also add expertise on subjects that you may not necessarily feel comfortable teaching by including guest trainers within your group.

Themed Content Calendar *(i.e.: #MondayMotivation, etc.)*

Monday:

_____

_____

Tuesday:

_____

_____

Wednesday:

_____

_____

Thursday:

_____

_____

Friday:

_____

_____

Saturday:

_____

_____

Sunday:

_____

_____

Conversations that Convert

Offering valuable content daily will keep your group engaged and allow you to nurture them from a cold lead to a hot prospect. Overtime, you will build up your know, like and trust factor. 90% of buyers need more time or more information before making a purchase or joining a business opportunity. Consistency will be your secret sales weapon.

Here are five ways to create more opportunities for conversations:

✔ *Create a Pinned Welcome Post*: You can do a post or go Live (*I recommend going Live if possible*) and pin it to the top of your group. You will want to share a bit about yourself quickly, why you created the group, and what they can expect by being a part of your group. Give them a Call to Action such as turning on the group notifications to All Posts.

✔ *Privately Message each New Member*: I truly believe this step can be one of the best long-term strategies when it comes to building real relationships with your group members and finding ways to serve them. Once accepted into the group, message them and say something such as, *"Hey NAME! So excited to have you in my group XYZ. What do you need the most help with?"* Then when they respond, tag them on something helpful in the group or put it on your schedule immediately to cover it as soon as possible if it is appropriate for your group.

✔ *Welcome New Members Weekly*: On a specific day of the week, use Facebook's™ tool to automatically welcome and tag all of the new group members from that week. You can also schedule these! This is such a great way to make sure everyone feels welcome and gives others the chance to say hello and connect.

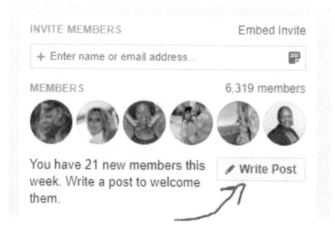

✔ *Acknowledge Your Most Active Members:* Rewarding members for being active in the group is a stellar way to make them feel seen but also to encourage others to up their game so they can be recognized as well. You could share updates weekly for the top contenders and reward them at the end of each month or even shout them out in your Stories. The possibilities are endless! Even a small token such as a cute notebook or a book goes a long way.

Members

Top Contributors ⑦

These are the top contributors from the last 28 days.

 1   Vicky Western Turner

✔ *Utilize Units so Newbies Get a Quick Win:* As you start to get your members answering questions in regards to what they need the most help with, bunch those topics into Guides so you can easily tag new members to get them started on the right path and realize the concrete value you are offering in your group. Make sure your group settings have Social Learning toggled on.

Selling Strategies

By being consistent with your content, interaction and conversations, you will create an engaged community that knows, likes, and trusts you. Remember that personal connection will always outperform automation in your Facebook™ Groups. It is absolutely fine to bring in a Virtual Assistant once you get things rolling but you need to be involved at the beginning stages of growth.

All of the content you share inside of your Facebook™ Group should be positioned so that what you are selling is eventually the next logical step. We don't want the goal to be to sell to our members or it will come across that way and you will find yourself posting and praying or worse, word vomiting. What you want to do is offer value that will help them solve a problem and what you have to offer is absolutely going to help them take it to the next level.

Let's say you're in the beauty industry and you sell cruelty-free makeup, you will want to share content that will help your members feel beautiful from the inside out. Then one day you could do a Facebook™ Live showing them some tips on how to make their eyes look bigger naturally with some makeup tricks and to let you know if they want info on the products you covered in the tutorial.

Another example would be covering your top ten favorite anti-inflammatory foods and while you are live say, "*And just drop more info below if you want to know what I take to supplement my diet and 10x my results when it comes to reducing inflammation.*"

Similar to your personal profile on Facebook™ or Instagram™ , you will want about 80% of your content to be neutral or value-driven and the rest can be positioned to work in your products, services or opportunities.

Everything I have been covering is intended for a value-based group as I know most of you will need to work on growing this primarily. For your customer-based group, you can have most of the content be about testimonials, products, promotions and success stories about the opportunity. Members know they are in there to learn about your company so it doesn't need to be as covert.

For your bigger ticket offers such as giveaways, challenges, and freebies, look for ways to make your offer the obvious solution. If you do a *Get Trim Challenge*, of course participants will want to get on your weight loss products to skyrocket their results, right? Here are a few more examples:

Meal Plan Giveaway ☐ *Nutrition Supplements* ☐
5 Day Instagram™ Challenge ☐
Instagram™ Content Planner ☐
Personal Branding eBook ☐ *Coaching Program* ☐

Ideas:

_____

_____

_____

_____

_____

_____

_____

_____

_____

_____

When it comes to selling successfully, you shouldn't have to "*sell*" anyone anything. If they have a real pain point and you have a real solution, it is just a matter of them getting to know you well enough or feel comfortable purchasing from you or joining your team. Be clear on how it will help them improve their life in the appropriate way. It should be a natural progression.

And remember to ask the question. Don't just hope people will reach out to you and ask to learn more about what you do, although that will absolutely happen if you follow what we have covered in this book so far. If someone comments that they are exhausted all the time and you see it in your group, reach out to them. *"Hey there, I hope you're doing great. I saw your comment in the group about feeling exhausted all the time and that was definitely me a couple of years ago. I switched things up a bit and now have more energy than I can handle. I'd love to get you some details on what I did. If not, no worries, I'll see you around the group!"*

One other situation I want to mention is, if you have other network marketers in your group and you are also in network marketing, they are all still potential customer prospects even if they are in the same industry. For example, I order a few health and wellness products from a few friends such as essential oils and I am with a health and wellness company. You don't want to proactively try to recruit them to your

184

team but if they reach out to you, it is absolutely fine to share more about what company you are with and why.

Selling takes time but when you get this skillset down, you will have way more fun in your business and you won't feel so lost. You will have purpose when you get onto social media and learn to get really great at converting conversations into sales. Lead with massive value and you can never go wrong!

CHAPTER 9

Leveraging the Loyal

"Here is a powerful yet simple rule. Always give people more than they expect to get."

~ Nelson Boswell

Dazzle with Excellent Customer Service

No matter what industry you're in, one of the biggest mistakes entrepreneurs make is working so hard to get a new customer, but doing nothing to retain them. As long as you have a consumable product or service, you can build up a true residual income with repeat customer orders and referrals.

Another key element when it comes to acquiring and retaining customers is to realize that most people are not great at recruiting. So, if you or people on your team can develop strength in excellent customer service, then overtime this can equate to massive amounts of referrals and many upgrades where they eventually decide to do the business.

No matter if you love leading with the business versus the product, you'll want to make sure you're implementing the steps in this section to take great care of your customers and to help your team do the same.

As soon as you get a new customer, immediately write them a handwritten thank you note and drop it in the mail. When was the last time you received a real thank you note in the mail? You will instantly stand out to your customer and they will appreciate the gesture. I have seen people make a personalized gift to go above and beyond, so consider that if you are more on the crafty side.

It is so important to have amazing customer service and take care of your new customer right off the bat. Are there any important FAQs or instructions you can either tag them on in a group or email to them directly? Can you opt them into an automated drip campaign via email, a texting service or ManyChat? Make sure they know how to get in touch with you if they need anything.

I find most of my students want to take good care of their customers, but they honestly just forget and don't do a good job of staying organized. Create a scheduled follow-up system so you know how frequently to check-in with them and make sure you don't space out on them.

Every so often, try to check in as a friend. You can make a Facebook™ Friends List with just your customers and periodically love on their newsfeed. Or shoot them a casual message from time to time and of course say happy birthday when the time comes!

Remember that your job is to reach out to them, not the other way around. Set them up for success when they first begin consuming your product or service and they will be way more likely to give referrals or share with others. People remember how you make them feel, not what you say.

Rock a Customer-Based Facebook™ Group

It is important to have a place to ATM your customers when necessary. If you aren't familiar with the term ATM in this context, it simply means *Add* them to a Facebook™ Group, *Tag* them on something inside the group, and then *Message* them that you did so.

There are a few different routes you can take with a customer group. You can have a traditional one that is just for customers, full of content about how to use the product, sales, etc.

Another option is to have a customer prospect group, which is where you put any potential customer and all current customers. This group would also have info on the product, but be heavier on the testimonial side and incentives to sign up as a customer.

Yet another option is to have a value-based group, where most of the content is geared towards what your potential customer needs help with or would improve their life. Examples would be groups around living a healthier lifestyle or how to feel more beautiful from the inside out.

You can have the group be 100% value-driven without mentioning your products or services at all, or you can follow the 80/20 rule. This is where 80% is value-based and the rest is utilizing curiosity and challenges to work in your products or services.

I have either run or had clients add me to all variations and I personally recommend starting with a value-based group and then plugging new customers into an upline's customer group. If they don't have one, you can create one later, but wait until you have a large enough pool of current customers to justify it, otherwise it could be quiet as a mouse and backfire.

No matter which way you go with it, you will want to make sure you, your teammates or a VA are planning content to be posted daily. I recommend going live weekly and adjusting the content until you truly get the hang of it.

In addition, you can infuse a lot of excitement into your customer-based group by doing raffles, challenges, and online parties. I would do these *no more* than once a month and change them up frequently so that you can keep them guessing...and engaged.

How to Run a Referral Blitz

As covered previously, learning how to gain referrals through your current prospects and customer list is extremely powerful. To really turbocharge your results, work in periodic referral blitzes for you and your team.

For a designated period of time, ideally three days, reach out to all of your prospects and customers and invite them to enter a giveaway. By posting on their wall for you, they get entered, no purchase necessary.

Make sure you are clear on when it ends and to actually pick a winner. I pre-determine the dates each month for my team and we always do a working Zoom to kick off the blitz and get everyone into massive action.

Average 30 New Warm Leads with Facebook™ Parties
Online events have also been previously covered, but let's break this down a bit more here and really talk about coaching your hostess and making the most of your 15 Minute Facebook™ Parties.

First off, don't assume your customer doesn't want to host one for you. I'll never forget working with a private client who was with a direct sales company that is heavy on parties and she wasn't booking any. When I had her run through her current customer list with me, she had an excuse for each one, but hadn't asked any of them. Right then and there, I came up with a script for her and made her message a few of them. Within an hour she messaged me, "*Omg, she said yes! Now what do I do?*" LOL. That is a good problem to have. If they say that they are busy right now and to circle back, you need to do just that. I know it can be uncomfortable asking for something, but make it worth their while and follow up. My best parties came from a strong follow up game.

Reach out to your prospective hostess and say, *"Hey, NAME! I wanted to see if you'd be willing to host an online party for me – of course I'd gift you with some product credit as a thank you! Mine are short and sweet (15 minutes) and then I'd just keep it open for 48 hours. Can we set something up?"*

Once you secure a time and date, be very clear on the hostess' expectations. Give her a script for inviting and check-in with her every day or so depending on how far out the party is and how many new group members are being added.

Schedule your posts ahead of time and ask her to comment on them and be active inside the group. Remember, not everyone is on social media all the time like us so they may not understand how important engagement is.

Let her know to tag her guests when you go live if she isn't seeing them commenting. This is a really big step that can make a big difference. Have her put anyone interested into a three-way chat with you and handle the rest for her. Keep her updated on sales and reward her with some kind of sales incentive, such as more product credits.

Keep track of all of your party participants on Trello or something similar and privately message all of them as the party is closing. Having a strong party incentive can help you close more sales for sure, so create some urgency!

And last, don't forget to reward your hostess and follow through with whatever you promised her. Reach out to all of your party guests that actively participated and see if they would host their own party to earn product credits for themselves.

Even with one party a week and an average of 30 leads, you would be looking at well over 100 new leads monthly! And those are warm leads – they know you and they already know the product. It is truly genius so make this a part of your Goal Digger game plan.

Upselling Happy Customers
Let's start with the dirty word that gets so many into trouble when it comes to upselling prospects or current

customers...*kitnappers*. If you haven't heard this term before, it refers to anyone who signs up to become a distributor without the intention of building the business. It is almost always because they want to get a discount on the enrollment kit. Sound familiar?

This is such an epidemic that some teams get huge surges of business from capitalizing on low kit fees and blasting it out to their prospect lists and on social media. As you can probably tell I am *strongly* against building a business this way.

It is confusing to the "new" distributor, as now you have to decide whether or not to plug them into your onboarding process. It can be extremely awkward. And this false spike in volume can create unsustainable rank advancements that cannot be maintained the following month and can cause a mental landslide.

In my opinion, the proper way to upsell a prospect or current customer is to tell them what is involved with becoming a business builder and ask if they'd like to upgrade. Never mention getting a discount on the product pack, focus on all the other perks.

When I have a hot referral post that is doing well and the comments are rolling in, I will reach out to the person who put the post up for me and tell them where I am with potential customers. If I am going over pricing, I will ask them if they want me to share my link with their referral or if they want to upgrade and earn the commissions themselves?

The cool thing is they are literally learning how to build their business on social media even before they start!

Another key place to ask is during your hostess's 15 minute Facebook™ party. While the party is open, if anyone is put in a chat with you or comments that they want more info on ordering, ask the hostess if they just want referral credits for hostessing or would if they like to upgrade so they can earn commissions on any sales from the party.

Again, if they upgrade, this party has become their launch event. Boom!

And lastly, for customers that are consistently ordering or you've had them for several months, maybe even years, ask them if they would like to look at the business side. Tell them clearly they love the products, would they like to learn how to be paid for sharing right on social media?

Don't assume. Ask.

The best part about the upsell process is you can definitely build a solid team even if you're not a great "recruiter," but tend to get customers much easier.

That is your funnel...get new customers, nurture, maximize their network for referrals, and upsell. Rinse and repeat!

CHAPTER 10

Love Your Ladies

"Leadership is a two-way street, loyalty up and loyalty down."

~ Grace Murray Hopper

Leadership is Learned

"A leader is one who knows the way, goes the way and shows the way."

~John C. Maxwell

"Leadership is not a position or title, it is action and example."

~Ancient Proverb

"If your actions inspire others to dream more, learn more, do more and become more, you are a leader."

~John Quincy Adams

Alright, Goal Digger! It is time to embark on the beautiful topic of leadership. I don't know about you, but for many of my students, this can be an intimidating or anxiety-ridden area of their business. It absolutely doesn't have to be because leading can be learned.

Yes, some do naturally lead better than others, but that just means you have to dig in a bit more…so what? It doesn't matter how long it takes you to feel comfortable leading others, just that you do put intention and focus around developing this critical skill set. It doesn't matter what niche or space you're in when it comes to your business, even if you're in more of a servant role, such as a VA, you are always leading others.

The saying, *"Your vibe attracts your tribe,"* is not just a catchy slogan, but a true reflection of your leadership style. We're all leading, whether we realize it or not. When the girls were toddlers, they would walk around saying, *"Oh, gosh!"* just like I do! The good news is that if the energy of your team isn't how you'd like to see it, you can change it! It's a blessing and an honor to lead others, and for you to be reading this book shows you are committed to learning and growing. It will feel uncomfortable at first but it is SO rewarding and definitely an amazing responsibility.

I was just listening to a training on neuroscience, and it was saying that *integrity* and *warmth* were the two requirements of a strong leader. I think sometimes when we think of a strong leader we think of someone laying down the velvet hammer, but that doesn't necessarily lead to retention.

Whether you're leading a team or privately coaching, retention is everything. I don't have the biggest team in my company but our numbers are always at the top of the leader boards because our retention is through the roof. Learning how to make everyone feel welcomed and valued is something you can all do. Don't just focus on the high performers. They are only a small percentage, just as you are.

We will get into characteristics of a leader next, but first, let's dive into a self-analysis to see where you're currently at when it comes to leadership. Be honest in your answers as this is just a moment in time. This exercise isn't for you to feel bad about yourself or your leadership abilities. This is so you can acknowledge where you are and improve.

You can ask a few of your team mates that you trust or maybe a trusted friend as you go through these questions and get their honest feedback. Tell them you don't want them to be nice, you want them to be truthful so you can grow as a leader.

There is always room to grow, so let's get started!

If I had a chance to ask your team mates or customers/clients what their experience is with you when it comes to communication, follow through, and overall feeling supported, what would they say and why?

_____

_____

_____

_____

_____

In what ways have you led others, whether it be a personal situation such as raising children, or in a work environment?

_____

_____

_____

_____

_____

_____

Do you enjoy leading others? Explain.

_____

_____

_____

_____

_____

_____

In what ways would you like to improve when it comes to leadership?

_____

_____

_____

_____

_____

Let's review essential traits you'll want to work on developing:

The Common Characteristics of a Leader (*adopted from The Huffington Post*)

1. *Collaborative*: Just like we discussed, leadership is about including others, no matter their level of activity or ability. Look for ways to make sure you

are creating a culture that is warm and inviting, of course keeping it positive. When working with your team or client base, find ways to recognize them all in different ways. Could you shout someone out for a great post they did? Is there a client who had a win that you could recognize on your wall? If you are achievement-oriented, this can be unnatural, so become systematic in your efforts if needed.

2. *Visionary*: The leader is responsible for constantly painting the vision, talking about the possibilities, painting the picture of a bright and better future. Often, individuals don't have a vision for themselves, they get bogged down in the daily grind. Be the kind of leader that sees more in them than they see. Speak potential to them. Always talk about where your team is going or the industry as a whole if you are in the coaching space.

3. Influential: You have influence over others. Whether you have one follower on Facebook™ or a team of thousands, you are constantly influencing others. This is why the responsibility of a leader is so high, because you are persuading others all the time and often not realizing it. Think about the choice of your words, content, messages, Facebook™ Lives or any

other avenue of communication you are utilizing and choose wisely.

4. *Empathetic*: A leader is empathetic, which doesn't mean coddling people's excuses, it means they try to put themselves in that person's shoes and be understanding. If you are a red personality, super driven and maybe even a little bossy, this will be a character trait you will want to focus on. Get on board or get out of my way is *not* a good leadership quality. Again, you don't have to coddle others or let them live in a victim mentality. Just acknowledge what they're going through, remind them of their why, and help them come up with a plan to get back on track.

5. *Innovative*: Be the type of leader who is constantly trying new things to improve…be open minded to ideas that are brought to you. Stay engaged in coaching and training so you can bring fresh ideas to your team. This is a great recruiting tool no matter what field you're in because it is very appealing to prospects.

6. *Grounded*: If you are all over the place and winging it constantly, you are going to isolate a large number of people following you or working with you as this

dissolves the character trait of integrity. Be grounded. Stand for something. Be consistent. Show up every day. Follow through and *always* do what you said you were going to do, even if you don't feel like it.

7. *Ethical*: This is kind of obvious, but be ethical. Following through and being reliable is a piece of this, but don't be one of those leaders who encourages bonus buying or shady reimbursements with kitnappers. Anything unethical will not only shoot you in the foot later, it will destroy any trust you had with that person, even if they don't say it. Think long term.

8. *Passionate*: A leader is passionate, excited, and energetic. You are the one responsible for rallying up the troops. Even if you're facing something negative with the current economy, or let's say *out of stock* issues with your company, you need to be the cheerleader. You need to remind everyone why you do what you do. Remind them of how you are helping people, changing lives and eventually changing their own lives and their families.

Common Mistakes to Avoid

Most everyone that gets into leadership gets there by default; meaning, most don't have formalized training in this area. Without proper guidance or coaching, it is VERY easy to make these common mistakes. So, if you've experienced any of these issues, it's okay – don't beat yourself up. Remember that hindsight is 20/20 and your goal is to continue to grow every single day, personally and professionally, and to inspire others to do the same! Now let's take a look at the most common mistakes:

Ignoring issues. When something happens with one or more of your teammates or clients, you need to address it head on. Avoiding it and hoping it will go away will not work and it can potentially blow up in your face. For example, if you have someone being negative in your team chat, redirect them publicly in the team chat so everyone knows what is or isn't appropriate and then send them a DM to go over proper etiquette.

One amazing strategy I learned early-on in my leadership days, two decades ago (*wow, that makes me sound ancient LOL*), was the sandwich management technique. Read *The One Minute Manager* for more details, but basically you will start with something positive, address the issue, then close with something else positive.

For example, let's say you have a team member who keeps texting you over and over again telling you they have someone in a three-way chat and asking you to please go in there. You could say, "*Jane, I absolutely love your eagerness to grow your biz and that you are utilizing three-way chats because they are awesome. However, you will want to set the expectation up with the prospect that I am a busy mom and may not be in right away but that's the beauty of Messenger – we can get to it when we have time. Again, love how hard you are working and I know it will really pay off for you!*"

Causes dependency. For my yellow personalities or recovering people pleasers, this one may hit home for you. If you are the only one who can onboard new team mates, you're doing all the three-way chats for your team, you're doing everything for your new coaching client instead of empowering them to do it, then this may be causing dependency. As a leader, your goal is to coach, inspire, and develop up-and-coming leaders that not only can do what you currently do, but surpass you. Whenever someone asks you for something, don't just send it to them. Tell them how to find it or access it.

Gives more than is receiving back (within reason). If you are running all the team meetings, contests, challenges, posting in your team's prospecting group...or any of the other millions of things that go into your business, and no one is reciprocating, this can cause resentment and make it easy for you to be taken advantage of. What I would recommend is asking for help. When you put your monthly calendar together for your team, ask who can run some of the Zooms. Or if you are hosting a challenge, ask for volunteers. If you don't get any traction, then stop offering to run those unless it is detrimental to your personal business.

Assuming their new people have "got it." If you are a natural jump-in-and-learn-by-doing kind of person, really pay attention to this one. Although you would assume people know what to do when they're new, they don't. Spell it out for them. *"Hey, Sarah! I'm so excited to have you on board. I just added you to our team Facebook™ page where your initial training will take place. Once you're in, let me know and I'll tag you on your first training video."* Once she does, tag her on it and say, "*Start here and then head to Guides 1-3. Tag me when you get to #2.*"

Doesn't set clear expectations. Set up boundaries right away but also get clarity from them on what their time commitment is weekly and income goals. I can't tell you how many times a leader will come to me frustrated that their awesome new Rockstar isn't doing anything when they could be crushing it. You can't choose their goal for them, they have to.

In regards to boundaries, I always let newbies know the best way to access me and the resources we have for them to be successful. They can typically find anything they need by searching our team Facebook™ group or asking in our chat. If it's something personal, they can come to me, but otherwise, they need to access what we have in place. This way they learn how to be efficient so they can teach their recruits the same thing.

Are bossy. I'm definitely more on the bossy side, ask my husband, but as a leader you want to ask and empower your people instead of telling them what to do. You can coach them to the results they need to be successful but walk them through the thought-process. If you are bossy and just tell people what to do, they will leave or not respect you.

Pushing people into ranks. Don't even get me started on this one, HA! But in all seriousness, don't push people into ranks. Ask them each month for a doable goal and a stretch goal. Check in mid-month and then weekly to close out and ask them if they want to run and go for the bigger goal, if appropriate. Ask them, don't tell them. If you do, they won't be behind the goal for whatever reason and will feel like they let you down. Also, if you push them into it with anything sketchy like bonus buying, they will not maintain that rank the next month and be starting behind the previous month because of all of the false volume you generated.

Feeds into negativity and drama. I know it's difficult, but you cannot talk about your downline to anyone outside of your upline. Go up. As a leader, your people need to know they can trust you and if you are talking about others that trust will go out the window. Squash the drama immediately. Address it head on, redirect wherever needed and don't tolerate it.

The bottom line is, lead from the front and always do the right thing, no matter how hard it is. If you're not sure what to do, find a mentor or someone in a similar place to lean on during those tough situations where the path is unclear.

I was lucky enough to participate in a program that John Maxwell rolled out specifically for leaders in network marketing. He wrote a book called *The Power of 5 for Network Marketers* and I recommend it to everyone. It is not sold in stores so just grab my link inside of the book resources section!

Developing a Team

When you hear the phrase "*developing a team*", this means learning how to teach your people to turn around and teach their people. This is the heart of duplication. You can do everything yourself if you try, but it will only get you so far in your business. And it is very stressful! Give people a chance to rise up and you will be amazed at what happens. Let's expand on the key areas to master.

Onboarding: The moment you get that new recruit, what you do next is critical, not only for their chance at success, but also for the quality of life you create and the time you spend on your business. In my opinion, you most definitely need to incorporate an automated onboarding system. This is so important that we have an entire module dedicated to teaching you how to set it up inside of The Academy. Whatever you do with them during that initial launch, they are going to subconsciously ask themselves if they want to dedicate that kind of time to growing their own business.

Keep it simple. Create systems you can plug them into that do not take a lot of your time. It's pure magic.

Launching: While they are launching their business, you are going to want to get them into activity and winning as soon as possible. My personal goal is to have every new recruit getting their first rank advancement before their product kit arrives. Your model and goal may be different but the only way to make it happen is to get them going. Getting that first customer will make them see they can do this. Again, keep it simple.

Duplication: When you look at the model you have set up, ask yourself, if you launch 20+ people at once and they all start bringing people onto the team, would it be able to get all of those people up and running successfully? This is a fantastic barometer for the health of your duplication model. As mentioned before, you cannot be all things to everyone on your team. Setting up your launch plan in a way that allows one person to come in and turn around to bring in another no problem means it is set up correctly.

Before I automated the 15-minute Facebook™ launch events, I happened to watch someone's live that was new and a few levels down. It was a train wreck. You could tell they were nervous, but the information was completely wrong. Take a peek at the different areas of your business and do some auditing to see that everyone is receiving the correct information and can access what they need to be successful.

Also, remember to redirect anyone who comes to you with questions to tell them where to get the answers. Remind them that you want to teach them to be resourceful so they learn how to protect their own time as they grow their organization.

Taprooting: One thing to always keep in mind, whoever joins your team likely does not understand leadership and probably isn't aware that they have the skills they need to develop. There are going to be more times than not that someone joins in your downline and has zero guidance. This can be detrimental for your team and also for their experience with your company.

To proactively address this, implement a taprooting system. This is where you reach down into your downline "tree" and mentor those that are raising their hand that they want to run or do not have someone properly leading them. Do what you can to work with their direct upline so that they can learn how to develop people under them. However, you will quickly learn who wants to rise up and who doesn't.

I like to reach out to every single new person that joins my team and introduce myself. Then I check my numbers daily to see who's truly working the business or who needs support and I *unapologetically* mentor wherever I can.

Also, towards the end of the month, I will see who is close to bumping up to a higher commission rate or close to a rank advancement through my back office reports. I will go directly to the person I want to communicate with and let them know because it can't hurt for them to have two people checking in with them!

And one other note I want to mention is to make sure you are connecting periodically with your direct reports throughout the month. You don't want to be that person reaching out at the end of the month asking where they think they will close out at. It's distasteful and I have experienced it first hand. Don't view people as a number, treat them with care and they will be very loyal and an integral part of your team's success!

Team Recognition

Because we are all so busy, I think recognition is often an afterthought or super last minute. How would it feel to get ahead of your incentives and actually think them through?

If you are achievement-oriented or tend to focus on just the results, you will most likely gravitate towards recognizing only those who perform. This is important and we do want to focus on this, but it cannot be the only thing you are recognizing. For example, recognizing the top ten in sales month to date at the beginning of each team meeting will make the 80%ers feel less than.

Instead, also recognize activity. This will allow everyone to feel seen and heard and appreciated for their hard work.

Sometimes results take longer for some than others and you don't want to lose people just because you aren't acknowledging them for how hard they are trying.

By including both results and activity throughout your incentive plan, you will be offering areas of motivation for everyone on your team. You will also notice some go from getting recognized for high activity and move into actually getting results, which is so rewarding.

And if one of your high performers slides backwards in results but keeps up their activity, they will be positively reinforced versus kicking themselves and quitting. It's a win-win!

When to Start Leading

You can start leading immediately and I want to encourage you to lean into it. Even if you don't have a team going yet, you can find ways to offer value inside of groups or within your social media efforts. If you've outgrown your own upline's leadership or have a different leadership philosophy, you can branch off and start your own Facebook™ group and/or weekly team calls. It takes quite a bit of effort to run either of these so don't do it just to do it.

Make sure you can commit to the consistent effort it takes to launch these and keep them going.

The summer before college, I took a sales job with Cutco Cutlery knives. I was super coachable (*are you surprised, LOL*) so not far into it, our manager asked me to start doing ride-alongs. I would bring a brand new person with me and they would just watch me to learn how I was getting results. They also learned how to build rapport quickly with people I didn't know, how to keep things moving along and how to close sales (*aka: how to sell very expensive knives to housewives, hehe!*).

In our time together in the car, we got to know each other. I would find out why they started selling knives which also was telling of their future goals and dreams. I would give advice and encourage them as they got going with their own presentations and mentor wherever I could. Although I was barely old enough to drive, I was leading others.

Anything new feels uncomfortable. But so does anything worth doing for the first time. You've got this. Now go help others and change the world.

CHAPTER 11

Making it Rain

"People don't buy because what you do is awesome.

People buy because it makes them feel awesome."

~ Tara Gentile

Why You Need an Awesome Lead Magnet

Depending on how long you have been an entrepreneur, you may be brand new to lead magnets or you may think that you don't need one. Either way, you absolutely need a lead magnet, and you need to learn how to make an awesome one. In this chapter, you will learn everything from how to create them, design them, and where to use them for maximum results.

If you are operating under the false pretense that social media is enough to generate and grow your business, I need to clear this up for you so you really are thinking like the marketer you are becoming. If you are building solely on social media, you are building your business on borrowed land. Think about it. If something happened to your account tomorrow or if your favorite platform had major algorithm changes or new rules, it could be game over for you.

This isn't to scare you. This is to help you see the value in building an email list, which you will do by learning how to create lead magnets. And you can also use lead magnets to fill up Facebook™ groups, challenges, free masterclasses and more! They are the cheapest, and in my opinion, the most effective way to get the ball rolling when it comes to true list building.

One common question I get is *"Does the lead magnet have to do with my product/service/opportunity?"* Yes and no. It doesn't directly have to, but there needs to be a path to connect the dots. For example, one of our Academy students used a free walking challenge to get leads for her beauty products by doing trainings inside the group she created talking about self-confidence and motivation...and it worked!

So there is nothing wrong with trying out a lead magnet not directly connected to what niches/industry you're in. Your main objective is to build up your know/like/trust factor with your new leads.

And in regards to email building specifically, remember, you own that list. If anything ever happens with your social media account or even your business, you can pivot much easier if you have an email list you have been growing.

The reason why lead magnets are so powerful is because there is a perceived exchange of value. When you have something someone wants, whether it be a cheat sheet, special training or a challenge to register for, your prospect is much more likely to turn over their email address to get what you have. And more importantly, they feel like they got something at the end of the day, right?

The feel of it is so much different than the typical online marketer's approach of take, take, take. With a solid lead magnet, you get to give! And that's where it starts to get really fun when it comes to building an online business.

Another great attribute of lead magnets is that they are truly evergreen content. What does that mean? Well, when you put out a piece of content such as a Facebook™ Live or a Story on Instagram™ , you get a day or two of shelf life and then no one really sees it again. But, with a lead magnet, it can be utilized over and over again as long as it is still relevant and aligned with your personal brand.

For example, I use bitly to track all my link clicks and my first lead magnet from three years ago has had about 25,000 clicks! That is pretty amazing if you think about the longevity but also the return on investment when it comes to the time I put into creating it.

Although you may not feel you have anything to offer when it comes to lead magnets, I can assure you that you do. And sometimes, the best lead magnets are the ones that you create to help yourself in some way or to repurpose content you have already created. They do not have to be anything fancy when you first start and as you will see, my first ones were a Word document saved as a PDF and with the power of Canva, yours will turn out way more professional than mine when I started.

But the bottom line is this: your prospects won't care what it looks like. They just want to know if it can help them in some way. If they perceive that it can, they will want it. Ready to get started?

What Makes a Good Lead Magnet?
There is a framework I like to follow when considering what type of lead magnet to create and what it will be about. Use

this as a guideline to get started but definitely trust the creative process or any inspiration you may uncover as you work through this material.

When I started my first business, *FitKim*, I made the rookie mistake of creating programs that I thought my audience wanted. I knew they would love it! But…I didn't actually identify what their specific pain points were to be able to know if I was truly solving a real problem that they had.

Flipping back to your notes, I want you to pull out your list of pain points you identified that your ideal avatar has. You can choose to focus on their pain points in relation to your product, service, or opportunity. I would start in the area you feel most comfortable with and that you know is their biggest need. You don't have to get this right the first time, so just choose. I would rather you take imperfect action than sit here and think about it too much.

From your list of all the pain points you have gathered, jot down a couple of the most urgent ones you feel that they are struggling with:

_____

_____

_____

_____

_____

_____

_____

_____

Now, on the flip side, I want you to brainstorm how you can offer a solution to those struggles (*ie: if their pain point was lack of time, you could come up with ways for them to get more organized*). Whatever you choose, it should be a quick and simple win, which is by definition the very nature of lead magnets:

_____

_____

_____

_____

_____

_____

Another element that is often missed and can really help your lead magnet convert is to consider your ideal avatar's psychographics. You can absolutely go the route of offering a tangible solution such as '*three ways to make your*

Instagram™ stand out'. But it can be just as powerful to think about how she is feeling, what her biggest challenges are, and what is truly holding her back. An example of keeping these needs in mind would be to create a seven-day morning mindset routine that she could follow to begin working on her own self confidence. Write down at least one idea for a lead magnet topic with this in mind:

_____

_____

_____

_____

_____

_____

_____

10 Different Lead Magnets that Rock

Now it's time to have some fun! In this section, I will share with you a ton of ideas that you can draw from to create your first lead magnet. As you go through these, circle the ones that jump out the most to you. Remember this is not the end all be all, you will be able to make more than one lead magnet as you go along.

Cheat Sheet

Think of a cheat sheet as your version of Cliffs Notes. When you were in school, most students would love to have been able to get their hands on the condensed version of the entire textbook, right? It is the same thing with a cheat sheet. If there is a seemingly complex task, you are going to give them a simple rundown or process to work through it easily. Honestly, people don't want to figure it out themselves often, so if you can make it a no brainer for them, they will opt in to receive it.

Checklist

Just like my Daily Activity Tracker PDF, you can organize tips into a checklist, tracker, or a list of some sort. These are also received really well because people are so busy they just love the simplistic format! In our fast-paced society, people also need help keeping things organized or working through a list so they follow through and complete the task at hand. You can really help people by making it easy for them to check off the boxes.

eBook

I know this sounds super fancy but it is as simple as putting together some helpful tips in Word, designing a cover in Canva and then saving it as a PDF. Voila! I also like to create a 3D image to promote it to increase the perceived value. My favorite site for that is *MyeCoverMaker.com*. If you notice that you tend to share the same type of things over and over again (*ie: recipes, craft ideas, etc.*), that is a good clue you have enough content for an eBook. Even if they are just a few pages, you can make them look really awesome.

Video Training

When you put together great content in the form of video training, why not reserve it for a special offer to your new subscribers? You can upload a Facebook™ or Instagram™ Live to YouTube/Vimeo or record one from scratch. Make the URL unlisted so that way it feels even more valuable to the receiver. When using this for a lead magnet, video series tend to do best such as "*My 3 Part Series on Learning* XYZ" You can space them out automatically via email so they don't receive them all at once.

Quizzes/Surveys

This lead magnet has a very high conversion rate because people are very curious – especially about themselves! One other huge benefit for creating a quiz or survey is that you can pre-qualify your leads and find out their pain points even before you talk to them. You may even discover they aren't truly a prospect and you can move on. This is a more advanced lead magnet so I would tackle this one later unless you are pretty tech-savvy. Google Forms or SurveyMonkey could easily work for surveys!

Webinar

If you want to do a deep dive on a specific topic that warrants more time than, say, a typical Facebook™ Live, scheduling and properly promoting a free webinar is an epic way to build up your email list fast. When you are setting it up in Zoom, check the box that requires participants to register. In the advanced settings after you create the Zoom, you can even add fields to the registration area to ask one or two more questions about your attendees. After you are done, even if they didn't attend live, you can access and download all of their email addresses!

Let your followers know that if they register for the webinar, they will get the replay as well as anything else important that you cover during the training. Once you have the replay uploaded and an unlisted URL generated, you can email out your list (covered later in this book) and also use it for a future lead magnet. See why I love webinars? I call mine masterclasses so whatever you refer to them as, make sure your audience knows they are free and encourage them to share it.

Templates

If you have created a framework that others can easily replicate or plug their info into and are off and running, this is called a template. An example would be all of the options you see in Canva for social media posts; those are templates. Templates really come in handy when it involves a creative process or any design work. You can really stand out with templates because SO many people struggle with anything tech-related so this can be a great one to choose.

Workbook

If you're reading this book, there is a high probability you have been in one of my challenges or attended one of my masterclasses and registered to receive your workbook. This is one of my favorite lead magnets because it gives your audience a solid reason to register and complete an action step before they even begin participating in your free offer. I love getting people into activity and I know it makes them feel good too. Workbooks are super simple to make so just refer to the eBook description above as a guideline.

Unique Content/Tutorials

This lead magnet would include anything specific such as a recipe, workout, DIY craft, etc. Let's say you do a cooking video and you could say to your viewers, "Just drop 'RECIPE' in the comments and I'll get this over to you." You would drop your lead magnet in the comments and they would have to complete that to get the recipe emailed to them. If you have a specific expertise, this can be a stellar lead magnet option for you and the perceived value is *very* high.

There are a ton of other lead magnets but this is a great starting point. Choose which one you'd like to start with and we will work on designing it in the next section.

Designing Your Eye-Catching Lead Magnet

We are so lucky because today it is beyond easy to create a beautiful lead magnet by using free software such as Canva. If you are more advanced, by all means use any design software you like, but for most of you, you can get the look you want by some basic skills shared in this chapter.

When I first started making lead magnets, I literally would design them on Word or Excel and save them as a PDF. My really old ones will probably give you a little giggle, but it got the job done and the email list going. As you grow, you can outsource this too if you find yourself not enjoying the process or struggling to find time making them.

With everything I teach, especially the more advanced stuff, I recommend you at least learn the basics, even if you're going to hire a professional. That way you understand the ins-and-outs and can communicate more effectively with your contracted professionals. I really do like designing lead magnets, but now Anna does most of them and let's be honest, she is *way* better at it than me, HA!

How & Where to Use Your Lead Magnet
Designing your lead magnet is an awesome accomplishment, but it isn't going to do you any good if you don't get it out there! Just like lead magnets themselves, there are a lot of different options, but I am just going to cover the ones I believe are most relevant to you and where you are currently at in your business.

❏ Facebook™ Profile Cover
❏ Facebook™ Bio
❏ Pinned Facebook™ Post
❏ Facebook™ Post

- ❏ Facebook™ Story
- ❏ Facebook™ Group Questions
- ❏ Facebook™ Group Cover
- ❏ Facebook™ Group Pinned Post
- ❏ Facebook™ Group Files Tab
- ❏ Facebook™ Events (*in description*)
- ❏ Message to New Group Members
- ❏ Facebook™ Live CTA
- ❏ Facebook™ Group Guest Training CTA
- ❏ ManyChat Welcome Menu
- ❏ Instagram™ Bio Link
- ❏ Instagram™ Post
- ❏ Instagram™ Story
- ❏ Instagram™ Live
- ❏ IGTV
- ❏ Reel
- ❏ YouTube
- ❏ Pinterest
- ❏ LinkedIn
- ❏ TikTok
- ❏ Milkshake/Linktree
- ❏ Project Broadcast

- ❏ Website Email Opt-In Landing Page
- ❏ Website Email Pop-Up
- ❏ One on One Messenger Conversations

CHAPTER 12

A Super Fan Brand

"It's easier to love a brand when the brand loves you back."

~ Seth Godin

What is Email Marketing?

Once you understand what email marketing is and what it isn't, you are going to start to see how powerful this strategy is and wonder why you waited so long to implement it. We will spend the majority of this chapter getting into the different types of email marketing, but first let's talk about the specifics of what it is.

Email marketing is not just sending an email to your list. The most common mistake I see with marketers just starting out in this arena is that they are inconsistent and send out random emails that have no rhyme or reason. If you do not have a strategy in place, by the time you send a second email, the receiver will have forgotten why they ever opted-in in the first place and unsubscribe right then and there.

The other common mistake is only emailing your list when you want something. The majority of your emails should be value-driven, just like your social media content. Otherwise, your subscribers will feel sold to and are much more likely to opt out of your list.

To prevent that from happening, you will want to implement true email marketing, which is what I will teach you in the rest of this chapter.

It is one thing to land in someone's Messenger, but to get into someone's email inbox, that is a whole other ball game. My favorite thing about my email sitting in another person's inbox is that they can get to it when they get to it. When I send a message on social media, they may open it and not want to respond or interact with whatever we are talking about within the conversation. So they don't reply, they move on, and they forget. But with an email, it is there waiting for them whenever they are ready.

The other powerful attribute to email marketing is that you are building up a solid relationship, one-on-one, with the receiver, and you are not on any social media platform. Unless it is an unusual circumstance, your email account is safe and the names on it are as well. It is yours. How amazing is that?

For the purpose of training on this, we are going to refer to the email marketing platform called Flodesk. I have used many others from basic to super advanced but I like their plug and play templates, they sync up to your Instagram™ feed and they look chic and modern. It is very intuitive and affordable as well. If you want something more robust, we currently use ConvertKit and I have friends that love ActiveCampaign.

Cold to Close Campaigns

We will focus on three different types of email campaigns during this chapter, and the first one is marketing to a cold list. You could create email campaigns to market to any of the emails you collect from the lead magnets we covered in the last chapter.

You may think it is going to take you eons to warm up cold leads but, when done well, you can start to build up trust *immediately*. Depending on what you are offering, you can even make a sale by the time they have opted into your email list. It really is powerful to be able to warm up a lead that quickly.

But before we email your new subscribers, we will need to create a basic landing page in Flodesk and sync it up to your automated email sequence. This comes first because even though you may not have your emails written right now, you are going to want to start collecting leads ASAP. This will put pressure on you to get them written when you get notified you have new subscribers!

To start implementing this, do a quick Google or YouTube search to see how to set up a landing page with Flodesk for your lead magnets. Look how cute this turned out and it took me two seconds:

Potential Customer Campaigns

This sequence is great to put into place as you collect email addresses from potential customers and new customers. You can tweak the messaging and segment the list into prospects and customers. I, personally, put them all on the same list to keep it simple.

We are mixing in value with mentioning the products and why they are so awesome. Having consistent messages going out automatically will save you so much time and really do the work for you when it comes to this format of built-in follow up!

In addition, you can also send a solo email or two to this specific list whenever you are having a flash sale. Your prospects and customers are way more likely to open up your email versus something from the company.

Nurturing the Committed Campaigns

The last type of email sequence we will explore within this program is the on-going, value-driven nurture campaigns. These are the ones you will be writing each week sharing organic content as you develop it. This isn't something you use over and over again. This is in real time. And your subscribers will love it.

You know how you follow influencers for so long that you feel like you know them? Or have you ever met one of your online mentors in person and felt like you'd already met previously? That is what these types of emails are going to do for the relationship you are building with your subscribers.

If you want awesome click-through-rates, get really good at showing up every week in the form of email. Even if it is a simple digest of the week or a short blurb of your weekly Facebook™ Live and a link to the replay, these are valuable beyond belief…yet many don't do them. They should not be an afterthought. They should be at the forefront of your marketing efforts.

Think Outside the Inbox
What I am giving you in this chapter is a very basic and simplistic way to get started with email marketing. You can get as creative as you want to, but the most important thing I want to emphasize is that I would rather you get something

out there and start capturing leads than spend hours on end making your landing page look beautiful.

Now as you go through this, if you are getting stuck to the point of frustration or you can tell it will be better to outsource, then you can definitely look into it. It does take time to find someone awesome who can do email marketing but there are plenty of amazing people who can really help you out if you need it.

Although it takes some time to get this set up and into action, think about all of this happening in the background, while you are doing other things to grow your business. That is how you leverage your time and quickly scale your business.

I am proud of you for being different and doing the things others won't do. Keep it up – I can't wait to see what is just around the corner for you.

CHAPTER 13

Stronger Together

"Surround yourself with only people who are going to lift you higher."

~ Oprah Winfrey

In closing, I want to encourage you to keep working on your life and pursuing your dreams, until you are living the life you've always envisioned. In that pursuit, I believe our greatest resource is to band together. I believe we make each other better. I believe we need an anchor to keep us connected to our dreams, and that anchor is the sister with her arm around you, telling you to keep going.

Lots of entrepreneurs have lofty ideas, but most quit. There are many out there that probably want the same thing you do, but they never overcome their fear of 'What-ifs" and never get started. They get stuck in paralysis analysis. They talk themselves out of anything that comes to mind and tell themselves to just forget it.

But not you.

You want more. And I know this because you picked up this book for a reason.

And I know in my heart that you *deserve* to have everything you want in your life and more.

You can make a difference in your home, as a mom, as a wife, as a person and you can make a difference in this world by building an incredible business full of passion and purpose.

You can inspire others.

You can empower others.

You can truly make a difference.

There will be setbacks and challenges, but as long as you have set clear goals that light you up, you'll come out on top.

You are resilient.

You are persistent.
And you have grit.

That is the magic formula, Goal Digger.

I used to live in fear. I used to doubt myself so much, I wouldn't even try anything new. I wouldn't take risks. I felt like an imposter.

And every morning I woke up with regret, knowing already before the day had even begun, that I wasn't going to pursue my dreams. I felt dead inside. My soul was barely a whisper.

But, I got help. I worked on my mindset *every* single day and began taking imperfect action. I decided I was never going to feel ready and gave myself permission to fail.

And that decision literally changed the trajectory of my life. I hope that you go back and read your favorite parts of this book again so that you are reminded you can do this. You are not alone. You have a tribe of #ElephantSisters and we have your back, during all the ups and downs of entrepreneurship.

So what is an #ElephantSister? This tribe was inspired by this beautiful story that has been floating around social media for quite some time. I stumbled upon it on Jen

Hatmaker's website. You can read the whole story on her site, but this is the theme:

On a particularly awful day, my ride-or-die friend Nichole Nordeman sent me a picture and a story. It was about female elephants, you know, as all good stories begin.

See, in the wild, when a mama elephant is giving birth, all the other female elephants in the herd back around her in formation. They close ranks so the delivering mama cannot even be seen in the middle. They stomp and kick up dirt and soil to throw attackers off the scent and basically act like a pack of fierce bodyguards.

They surround the mama and incoming baby in protection, sending a clear signal to predators that if they want to attack their friend while she is vulnerable, they'll have to get through forty tons of female aggression first.

When the baby elephant is delivered, the sister elephants do two things: they kick sand or dirt over the newborn to protect its fragile skin from the sun, and then they all start trumpeting, a female celebration of new life, of sisterhood, of something beautiful being born in a harsh, wild world despite enemies and attackers and predators and odds.

243

Nichole sent all this to me and said: We have you. You are never alone.

This is exactly what we do, girls. When our sisters are vulnerable, when they are giving birth to new life, new ideas, new ministries, new spaces, when they are under attack, when they need their people to surround them so they can create, deliver, heal, recover...we get in formation. We close ranks and literally have each others' backs. We do the heavy lifting while our sister is down. You want to mess with our girl? Come through us first. Good luck.

And when delivery comes, when new life makes its entrance, when healing finally begins, when the night has passed our sister is ready to rise back up, we sound our trumpets because we saw it through together. We celebrate! We cheer! We raise our glasses and give thanks.

David Yarrow Photography

If you are still searching for your tribe, please look up #ElephantSisters on Facebook™ or go to the book resources and join any of our Facebook™ Groups. We'd love to have you be a part of our community!

Cheers My Friend

It was an absolute honor to share this book with you. I know some of this work makes you feel very vulnerable and asks you to take some scary steps. I know this is just the beginning and my hope for you is that you continue to work on yourself because I believe in you, I think you're awesome and I know that you are absolutely worth it. We may not know each other personally, but we have been energetically attracted to one another, and because of that, I know your heart.

I've said this before and I'll say it again: it's time to stand up for your dreams. It's time to stand up for your happiness. It's time to fight for your life, look in the mirror and say, "*I want more. I demand more. I am creating more today.*"

I know you will do this and more, because you are a Goal Digger.

Goal Digger *[Noun]:* A driven person who's ready to #getLIT in her business, ignite her life, and set her soul on fire!
~ *Kimberly Olson*

ABOUT THE AUTHOR

Kimberly Olson is a self-made millionaire and the creator of *The Goal Digger Girl*, where she serves female entrepreneurs by teaching them simple systems and online strategies in sales and marketing. Through the power of social media, they are equipped to explode their online presence and get real results in their business, genuinely and authentically.

She has two PhDs in Natural Health and Holistic Nutrition, has recently been recognized as the #2 recruiter in her current network marketing company globally, is the author of four books including best-sellers, *The Goal Digger and Why Balance is B.S.*, has a top 50 rated podcast in marketing *and* travels nationally for public speaking opportunities.

Most recently, she has shared the stage with Rachel Hollis, Ray Higdon, Rob Sperry, Frazer Brookes and is an Ambassador for John Maxwell.

She is a busy mom of two and lives in Austin, Texas with her husband, Scott. Her favorite thing about being a mompreneur is being able to take care of her family while building an incredible business. And of course, she also loves teaching others how to follow their dreams, crush their goals and create the life they've always wanted.

Stay Connected

Her Courses: http://bit.ly/TheGoalDiggerVault

Facebook™ *@TheGoalDiggerGirl*

Instagram™ *@TheGoalDiggerGirl*

TikTok™ *@TheGoalDiggerGirl*

YouTube™ *@TheGoalDiggerGirl*

LinkedIn™ *@TheGoalDiggerGirl*

Twitter™ *@Goal_DiggerGirl*

Pinterest™ *@GoalDiggerGirl*

TheGoalDiggerGirl.com